CW00494149

BRITAIN
and the
GREAT
WAR

John Robottom

LONGMAN

Longman Group Limited
Longman House, Burnt Mill, Harlow,
Essex, CM20 2JE, England and Associated
Companies throughout the world

© Longman Group Limited 1996

All rights reserved. No part of this
publication may be reproduced, stored in a
retrieval system, or transmitted in any form
or by any means, electronic, mechanical,
photocopying, recording, or otherwise,
without either the prior written permission
of the Publishers or a licence permitting
restricted copying issued by the Copyright
Licensing Agency Ltd, 90 Tottenham Court
Road, London, W1P 9HE.

First published 1996

ISBN 0 582 08253 6

Set in 11/15pt Bodoni (Lasercomp) by
Keyspools Ltd, Golborne, Lancashire
Printed in Hong Kong

The publisher's policy is to use paper
manufactured from sustainable forests

Designed by Michael Harris
Illustrations by Tony Richardson and
Kathy Baxendale

We are grateful to the following for
permission to reproduce photographs:

Australian War Memorial, 27; British
Library (Newspaper Library), 95; from 'The
Bystander's' Fragments from France, 1916,
71 centre; Commonwealth War Graves
Commission, 87 right; E.T. Archive, 12, 19
top (both), bottom left, 42 right, 49; Mary
Evans Picture Library, 90; Illustrated
London News Picture Library, 66, 78;
Imperial War Museum, London, 7, 8, 14, 19
below right, 21, 25, 36, 37, 38, 39, 40, 42
left, 43, 46, 50, 54, 58, 60, 65, 68, 71 left and
right above and below, 76, 79, 84, 94; from
John Bull, 8 September 1917, British
Library (Newspaper Library), photo
courtesy of Shirley Seaton, 33; Historisches
Archiv Fried. Krupp GmbH, 15; Liddle
Collection, University of Leeds, 21, 61;
Musée de la Presse, Paris (Photo: Lauros-
Giraudon), 16; courtesy of the Director,
National Army Museum, London, 23, 82;
Peter Newark's Historical Pictures, 16;
Peter Newark's Military Pictures, 10;
courtesy Punch, 45; from Punch (7 April
1915), 63, (2 January 1918), 70; Science
Museum, London, 53; from The Times
History of The War, 1915, Vol. V. 13;
ZEFA, 87 left

Cover photograph:
'Are YOU in this?', recruiting poster, 1915.
This poster was designed by Lord
Baden-Powell, a distinguished soldier,
and founder of the Boy Scout Movement.
Imperial War Museum, London

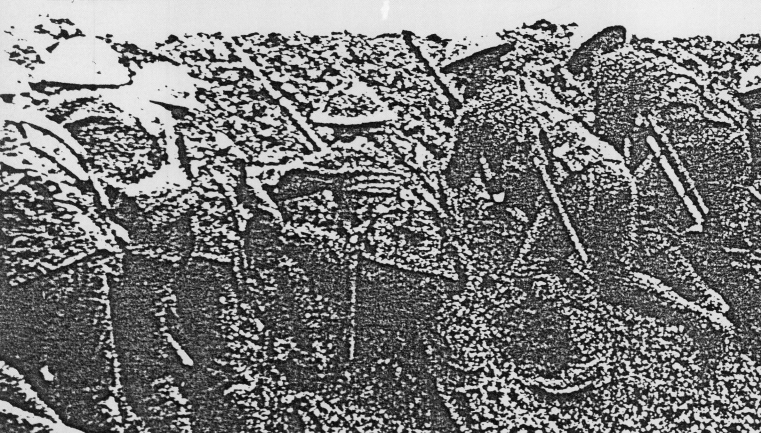

Contents

1
1914: decision time for Britain

In the circumstances that Great Britain is at war with Germany,

Act upon Instructions.

At 11 p.m. on 4 August 1914, Britain declared war on Germany. On 5 August, boys on cycles delivered 100,000 telegrams like this. Soldiers set off for their regiments. The police collected 120,000 horses from tram companies, delivery firms and farmers. Railway and shipping managers prepared 1,800 trains and dozens of ships.

On 17 August, soldiers of the British Expeditionary Force, or BEF, crossed to France. By 20 August, French trains took them to Mauberge on the border with Belgium (see map on page 8). There were about 100,000 men, around half of Britain's Army. All of them were trained, professional soldiers. Half of them were stationed in Britain for emergencies like this. The rest were kept overseas in Britain's colonies.

Mauberge is about 60 kilometres from Waterloo, where the British and German armies had defeated Napoleon, the Emperor of France, 99 years before. That was the last time a British army had crossed the Channel to mainland Europe. Why were they going in 1914?

Europe mobilises

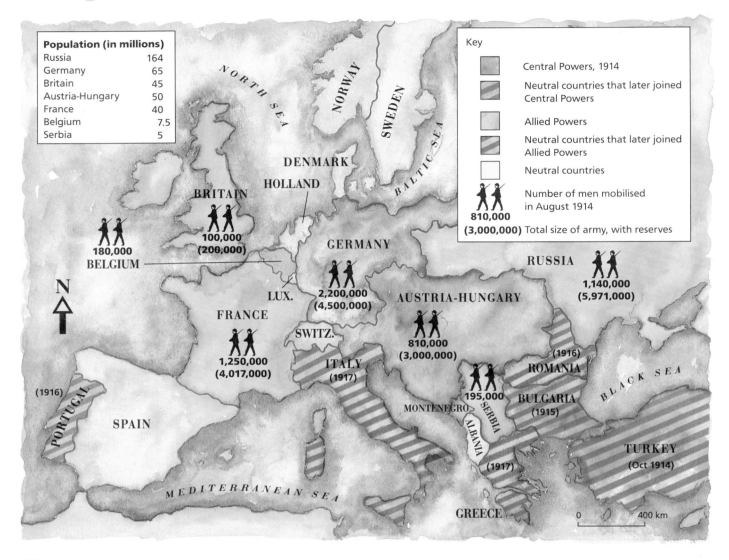

Population (in millions)

Russia	164
Germany	65
Britain	45
Austria-Hungary	50
France	40
Belgium	7.5
Serbia	5

Key

Central Powers, 1914

Neutral countries that later joined Central Powers

Allied Powers

Neutral countries that later joined Allied Powers

Neutral countries

Number of men mobilised in August 1914

810,000
(3,000,000) Total size of army, with reserves

BELGIUM
180,000

BRITAIN
100,000
(200,000)

GERMANY
2,200,000
(4,500,000)

RUSSIA
1,140,000
(5,971,000)

FRANCE
1,250,000
(4,017,000)

AUSTRIA-HUNGARY
810,000
(3,000,000)

SERBIA
195,000

NORTH SEA
NORWAY
SWEDEN
BALTIC SEA
DENMARK
HOLLAND
LUX.
SWITZ.
ITALY
(1917)
ROMANIA
(1916)
BULGARIA
(1915)
BLACK SEA
MONTENEGRO
ALBANIA
(1917)
TURKEY
(Oct 1914)
PORTUGAL
(1916)
SPAIN
MEDITERRANEAN SEA
GREECE

N

0   400 km

1 **Europe on the eve of war, August 1914.**

France was one of six European countries which had mobilised a large number of reserve soldiers and sailors to be ready for action between 31 July and 3 August.

In these six countries all men aged 17 or 18 were forced to spend two or three years in the army. Afterwards they became part of the 'reserve' which could be called up when their government decided to mobilise its forces. Since the 1890s, the army chiefs of each country had been up-dating their mobilisation plans. All plans depended on things like railway timetables, so they could not be changed easily at the last minute. For example, in 1914, France's mobilisation plans needed 7,000 trains to leave at eight-minute intervals, to move 1.25 million men. Germany's plan was even more complicated.

2 The order for mobilisation in France, 2 August. The poster says: *By decree of the President of the Republic, mobilisation of the land and sea forces is ordered, along with the requisition of animals, wheeled vehicles and harnesses needed to supply these forces.*

---

1 What does 'mobilisation' mean in everyday language (source 2)? What did it mean to the French Army in August 1914?

2 Which animals were most likely to be 'requisitioned' (taken over in time of emergency)? Why?

ARMÉE DE TERRE ET ARMÉE DE MER

ORDRE DE MOBILISATION GÉNÉRALE

Par décret du Président de la République, la mobilisation des armées de terre et de mer est ordonnée, ainsi que la réquisition des animaux, voitures et harnais nécessaires au complément de ces armées.

Le premier jour de la mobilisation est le *Dimanche deux août 1914*

Belgium was a neutral country so its soldiers were going to take up *defensive* positions on its frontiers, and at the huge forts at Namur and Liège. All other armies were planning to go on the *offensive* – to attack the enemy inside its own country.

---

3 Name the countries which mobilised for war in August 1914.

4 Several present-day countries do not appear on the map (source 1). Can you name them?

5 How does the map explain why Germany and its allies were called the 'Central Powers'?

6 How do you explain the difference in size between the armies of Britain and the rest of Europe?

7 Suggest reasons why Germany mobilised more men than any other country.

3 A poster by Jean Jacques Waltz (also known as Hansi). The quotation by Victor Hugo says: *This heaven is our blue sky. This field is our land. This Lorraine and this Alsace are ours.* The painter, Hansi, was born in Alsace in 1873.

1 The soldiers in the poster (source 3) are French. They are looking east. Which countries lie beyond the barbed wire?
2 What does the picture suggest is happening?
3 What is Hansi's view about this?

Why did war break out in Europe?

Long before 1914, there were trouble-spots in Europe where strong feelings could easily flare up. The two disputes most likely to lead to war were on the French–German border and in the Austro-Hungarian Empire.

The French–German frontier

The French would never forget their defeat and the loss of Alsace and Lorraine to the Germans in 1871. Until then, the French had formed the largest single nation-state in Europe. Although the Germans were greater in number, they were divided among five kingdoms. The largest of these was Prussia in the north. In 1870 the Prussian Chancellor, Otto von Bismarck, whipped up anti-French feeling among the German states. France fell into Bismarck's trap and declared war. The Prussian generals then led armies from all five German states into France. They won a crushing victory at the Battle of Sedan, and then forced the capital, Paris, to surrender.

It was a humiliating blow. France had to watch while the King of Prussia was proclaimed Emperor (or *Kaiser*) of a united Germany of all five kingdoms – in the French royal palace at Versailles. To get the Germans to leave, France had to hand over the lands of Alsace and Lorraine.

France's war plan from that time onwards laid down that their main army would march straight into Alsace-Lorraine. The French generals believed that a mobile army, not weighed down with heavy guns, would work best. Victory would come from *élan et cran* – fighting spirit and guts.

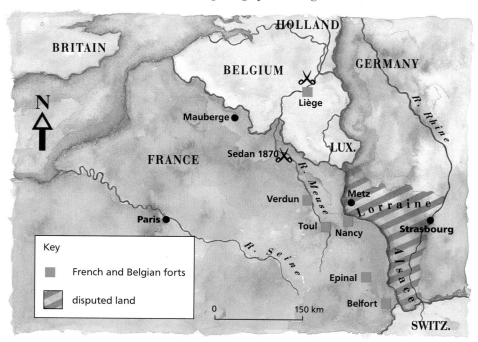

4 Franco-German border, 1914.

Austria-Hungary and the Serbs

There was another important trouble-spot in Europe. The Kingdom of Serbia had been fighting for seventy years. Its aim was to unite all Serb people living in the south-eastern part of Europe known as the Balkans. By 1913 only one large group of Serbs was still living outside Serbia. They lived in Bosnia, an area which was ruled by Austria-Hungary. Most Bosnian Serbs wanted to join with Serbia. Some had set up revolutionary groups inside Austria-Hungary which were secretly helped by officers in Serbia's army.

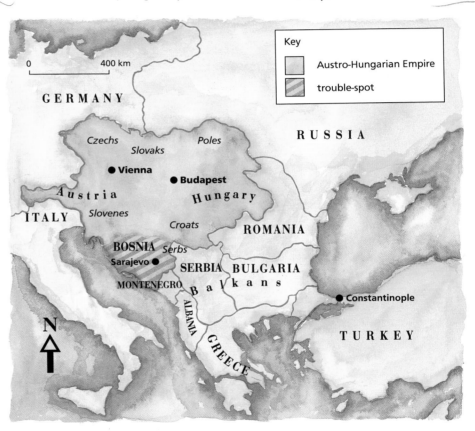

5 Central and south-east Europe in 1914.

As well as the Serbs, there were many other peoples, or nationalities, living in Austria-Hungary. Austria-Hungary was a large empire with two ruling nationalities – Germans and Magyars. The twelve million Germans (Austrians) had their capital in Vienna. The ten million Magyars (Hungarians) had theirs in Budapest. These two nationalities ruled over 23 million Poles, Czechs, Slovaks and other groups as well as Serbs. Many of these peoples wanted more freedom to rule themselves.

The Austro-Hungarian Empire had 48 army divisions. Serbia had just 11 if it fought on its own. But Serbia was allied to the vast Russian Empire. If Russia helped the Serbs in war, Austria-Hungary would have to send the largest part of its army north-east to defend its frontier with the Russian Empire.

6 | German and Austro-Hungarian soldiers advance side by side, 1915.

Assassination: the spark that led to war

The Emperor of Austria-Hungary was 84. His heir was Archduke Franz Ferdinand. On 28 June 1914 the Archduke and his wife visited Sarajevo, the capital of Bosnia. So did a group of Bosnian revolutionaries ready to die to free their people from Austria-Hungary. They had been trained in Serbia.

That morning one revolutionary threw a bomb at the royal car. It injured an officer. Later the Archduke and his wife went to visit him in hospital. Their driver lost his way in a narrow street. By chance, one of the plotters, Gavrilo Prinčip, was nearby. He shot and killed the Archduke and his wife.

Austria-Hungary's generals saw the assassination as 'a gift from Mars [the god of war]'. It gave a perfect excuse for war on Serbia. On 23 July, Austria-Hungary sent Serbia a demand that they must be allowed into Serbia to hunt down revolutionaries. Serbia was meant to turn this down, and it did. On 28 July Austria-Hungary declared war on Serbia.

This was no hasty decision. The Austrians had checked with Germany first, who said Austria-Hungary would have its full support. The two countries were allies and had shared war plans for twenty years. Germany's support meant that Germany was ready to fight Russia too if it came to Serbia's aid.

The Germany and Austria-Hungary alliance was not the only one in Europe. There was another important one between France and Russia. They planned to fight Germany together if it attacked one of them. By 1914 Europe was divided into two camps, each ready to fight the other. (See map on page 6.)

The Schlieffen Plan

The Russian–French alliance meant that the German war-planners faced a war on two fronts. They had to choose between fighting France and Russia together, or trying swiftly to knock one out first.

From 1891 to 1906 the German Chief of General Staff was Count von Schlieffen, who drew up a plan for a war on two fronts. Von Schlieffen planned for a knock-out blow against France first because it was more industrialised and heavily-armed than Russia. He calculated that most of the German army should strike west, and only a third would go east to hold off a Russian invasion. The main force would be in Paris in a matter of weeks.

The Schlieffen Plan put most strength into the right-wing armies which would circle round to take Paris, cutting the capital off from the sea. That meant going through Belgium. The Germans were not much troubled about invading Belgium except for one thing. Belgium was neutral. In 1839, Britain and the leading German state had signed a treaty saying they would protect Belgian neutrality (see source 9). So if Germany invaded, Britain might come to Belgium's aid. Some German leaders believed that Britain would not wish to get involved in a war and that she was more of a danger as a naval power than a land force. Ultimately the Germans decided to take the risk.

1 **What does this picture (source 6) suggest about the relationship between Austria-Hungary and Germany?**
2 **How would an alliance between Austria-Hungary and Germany link the trouble-spots in east and west Europe?**

7 The Schlieffen Plan prepared Germany for war on two fronts. The German Army would strike a speedy knock-out blow at France, before turning to war on the Eastern front with Russia.

Look carefully at source 7.
3 How well would the French armies be prepared to deal with these German plans?
4 What was the main risk in the plan for the Germans?

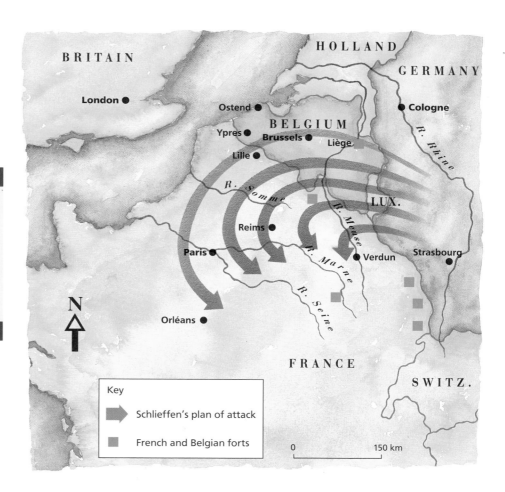

Key

➡ Schlieffen's plan of attack

■ French and Belgian forts

0   150 km

Britain decides on war

Britain ruled an empire on which, it was said, the 'sun never set'. To hold on to this vast empire, it had the world's largest navy. The British Army was much smaller than that of any other European country, but its soldiers were well-trained regular troops. Nearly half were stationed overseas in India, the West Indies, Africa, and smaller colonies and trading posts in every ocean.

Because of its island position and its empire, Britain had not felt the need to make alliances in Europe in the 1890s. Yet there was a growing worry about the rising strength of Germany. Since 1871 Germany had outstripped Britain in the production of steel, chemicals and electrical engineering. Its navy was catching up with Britain's too. It now had new super-battleships called Dread-noughts. German traders and soldiers were also opening up colonies in Africa and China.

12

As it had come to distrust Germany, Britain had drawn closer to France. In 1904 the two countries came to a friendly understanding, or *entente cordiale*. In 1907 Britain also came to an *entente* with Russia.

After the *entente*, British and French generals met often to share plans. Nothing was said in public about this, but they agreed in secret that if war broke out, the tiny British Army would go to the Belgian border while the huge French Army would march into Alsace-Lorraine.

The British Government and army generals were therefore ready for war in 1914. But on 2 August, when mainland Europe had mobilised, the British people were not so sure. The Prime Minister wrote to a friend that, 'a good three-quarters of our party in the House of Commons are for absolute non-interference'. Most MPs, like many other people in Britain, could not see why war in Europe should involve Britain. *Punch* showed their point of view in this rhyme:

> **8** *Why should I follow your fighting line*
> *For a matter that's no concern of mine?*
> *I shall be asked to a general scrap*
> *All over the European map,*
> *Dragged into someone else's war*
> *For that's what a double* entente *is for.*

Punch, July 1914

On 4 August, German troops crossed the border into Belgium. Suddenly, the issue seemed clear. Britain must help Belgium to defend its neutrality. The Germans must not be allowed to overrun its weaker neighbours. The British Government gave Germany an ultimatum: 'leave Belgium in twelve hours or we will be at war'. No reply came. War Office clerks stayed up all night stamping the 'Germany' into the telegrams which began to go out early next morning. A few weeks later the poster on the left was pasted on boards around Britain.

1 What did *Punch* mean by a 'double *entente*' (source 8)?

THE "SCRAP OF PAPER"

These are the signatures and seals of the representatives of the Six Powers to the 'Scrap of Paper'—the Treaty signed in 1839 guaranteeing the independence and neutrality of Belgium. 'Palmerston' signed for Britain, 'Bülow' for Prussia.

The Germans have broken their pledged word and devastated Belgium. Help to keep your Country's honour bright by restoring Belgium her liberty.

ENLIST TO-DAY

9 A recruiting poster. It shows a picture of the treaty signed in 1839, guaranteeing the independence of Belgium.

2 Look carefully at source 9. What does the 'scrap of paper' refer to? Why is it described as such?

3 What does 'guaranteeing' independence mean?

4 Suggest reasons why Britain had 'guaranteed' Belgium in 1839.

5 What reason does this poster give for Britain joining the war? From the information in this chapter, what other reasons might have been given?

The forces of war

Soldiers and weapons

What was a typical army like in 1914? An army was made up of up to ten divisions. Most divisions were *infantry* (made up of foot-soldiers), but there were also *cavalry* (made up of soldiers on horseback) and *artillery* (made up of soldiers who specialised in using large guns).

Most infantrymen fought with rifles and bayonets. For every 200 or so men there was also a four-man machine-gun section which could sweep 500 rounds a minute at the enemy. Cavalrymen rode into battle with rifles and machine guns. Their job was to rush through gaps made by the infantry and capture the ground beyond.

Riflemen and machine-gunners usually fought at ranges of a few hundred metres. But attacks could also start from further away, with shelling by the large guns of the heavy artillery. Light artillery guns were sometimes called 'field guns' because they were used on the battlefield. They fired shrapnel shells which were packed with bullets which exploded over the enemies' heads, killing many people.

Heavy guns were not easy to move, so they were fired from fixed positions. Their shells were packed with high explosive. The heaviest guns of all were built to fire at the massive steel and concrete forts which defended the frontiers in Western Europe (see source 7).

6 In 1914 it was important to have more horses and men in a battle than the enemy. How is this different from war in the 1990s?

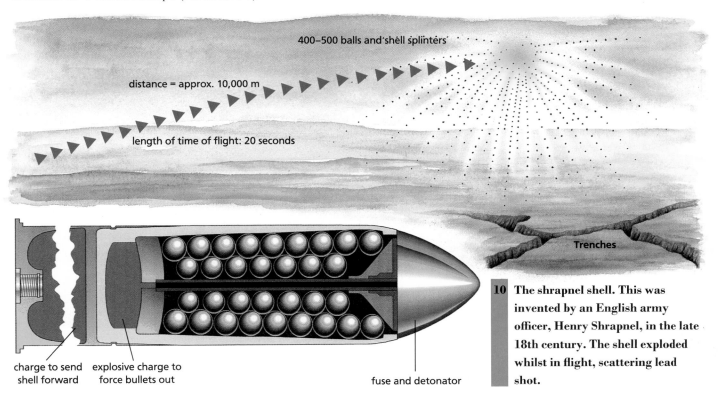

400–500 balls and shell splinters

distance = approx. 10,000 m

length of time of flight: 20 seconds

Trenches

charge to send shell forward

explosive charge to force bullets out

fuse and detonator

10 The shrapnel shell. This was invented by an English army officer, Henry Shrapnel, in the late 18th century. The shell exploded whilst in flight, scattering lead shot.

14

1 Which country had the greatest strength in artillery (source 11)?
2 How does source 12 suggest that the most advanced industrial countries could have the advantage in war?
3 What reasons would Germany's leaders have for believing they could win a European war?

Technology and war

The strength of a country's armed forces depended as much on technology and the industry that supplied them, as on the soldiers themselves.

11 Strength in guns, 1914

Type of gun	Germany	France	Britain
Light	6,000	3,800	200
Medium and heavy	3,500	300	100

By 1914, steel had been used for about fifty years. It was much stronger and more hard-wearing than the iron it replaced. It was widely used for making ships, machines, and bridges. Steel guns were also far more powerful than the iron cannons of fifty years before.

12 A heavy gun: a British 15-inch howitzer.

Engineering
accurately made parts

Steel making
different kinds of steel

Chemicals

high explosives

15 inches

charge

detonator

13 A Krupp steel factory in Germany, early twentieth century.

4 Suggest illustrations you could use to show the connection between industry and military power today.

Weapons and warships were made by a few leading steel companies across Europe. The greatest of these was the German firm of Krupp, which had 82,500 workers in sixteen steelworks and shipyards. It was more than twice as big as the French steel company Schneider, or the total of the two British firms, Vickers and Armstrong. Both of these British companies made far more guns for the Navy than for the Army, while for the German and French companies it was the other way around.

The chemical industry was also vital in war. The most powerful high explosive was TNT (**trin**itrotoluol) which was extracted from coal-tar. The same process was used for making artificial dyes. Before the war, nearly all dyes were made in Germany. Britain had the world's largest textile industry but it imported 90 per cent of its dyes from Germany – including the khaki colour for uniforms!

Nitrates were needed for the charge and detonator, and also to produce another explosive, AMOTOL. Nitrates were produced from saltpetre (potassium nitrate) which was imported from Chile. In 1909 a German chemist found a way of making nitrates from nitrogen in the air, using very high temperatures and pressures. This meant that Germany no longer relied on supplies of saltpetre which might be cut off in war. This gave Germany an important advantage over Britain and France.

The army generals knew how they would use the fifty-year-old technology of steel and chemicals in war. They were much less sure about three very recent technologies: motor vehicles (dating from 1886); aircraft (1903); and wireless (1897).

1 **What does this poster (source 14) tell you about how suitable aircraft were for war?**

2 **In 1914 all armies had more balloons for observation than aircraft. How does the picture suggest reasons why?**

3 **Can you work out the difference between 'puller' and 'pusher' aircraft?**

4 **Suggest reasons why armies made more use of technologies which dated back to the 1870s than those which were developed just before or after 1900.**

In 1913 there were about 300,000 motor cars, vans and trucks on British roads; the Army owned just 80. At the same time, a division of 18,000 infantrymen needed 5,600 horses to pull guns, wagons, field kitchens, ambulances, water carts – and their own oats. Despite the disadvantages, horses were still the main form of army transport when war broke out.

Wireless was already in use on all large ships by 1914, but the Army made much more use of an invention of the 1870s: the telephone. As they advanced, the Army would unroll kilometres of wire connected to field telephones.

From 1903 (when the Wright brothers made their first flight) to 1914, aircraft developed from being able to fly a few hundred metres to fifty or so kilometres. But just how useful would the new invention be in war? In 1914, the main use that generals could see for aircraft was to fly over the battlefield to observe enemy movements. No army general saw it as a fighting machine.

14 A poster for an exhibition of Europe's most advanced aircraft in 1909.

Review and Assessment

LATEST ORDERS
KAISER
OF THE
TO HIS GENERALS.

It is my Royal and Imperial command
that you concentrate your energies, for
the immediate present, upon one single
purpose, and that is that you address all
your skill and all the valour of my
SOLDIERS to EXTERMINATE
first, **the treacherous English,**
walk over General French's
contemptible little Army.

Headquarters Aix la Chapelle, August 19th, 1914

What answer must
Britons give ?

GOD SAVE THE KING.

B O MASON, Printer, 30 Frodsham Street Chester

15 British recruiting poster made
from the Kaiser's message.

1 Look at source 15. This British recruiting poster used the orders given by
the German Emperor to his soldiers as they approached the
Belgian border.
  a Give two reasons why the British were moving to the Belgian border.
  b In what way was it true that the British Army was 'little'?
  c Explain ways in which the British Army might not have been 'contemptible'
  (worthy of scorn) in battle.
  d Why did the Germans feel angry at Britain joining the war?
  e How did the position of the British interfere with the German war plans?
  f If General French, the British Commander-in-Chief, had known of the
  German war plans, what chance would he have given himself of winning the
  first battle?

2 Divide into six groups of soldiers moving to the Front: British; French;
Germans; Russians; Austro-Hungarians; and Serbs. In each group, choose an
'officer' who will explain why your country has gone to war. (Use a map if it is
helpful.) The other group members are soldiers who question their officer
about the dangers they are going into.

3 Historians have long argued about the causes of the Great War. Among other
things, people have blamed:

  (i) the aims of German political leaders and generals;
  (ii) the system of alliances;
  (iii) the fact that war plans were fixed and could not be altered;
  (iv) the wish of people who produced weapons to make bigger profits;
  (v) the fact that Germany invaded France through Belgium, not Alsace-
  Lorraine;
  (vi) the strength of nationalist feelings, especially in France and Serbia;
  (vii) the fact that Britain did not make it clear that it would fight until war had
  begun.

  a Write down what you would say in support of each of these views.
  b List them in *your* order of importance. (Remember: there is no correct
  order.)
  c Give your own explanation of the causes of the war. If possible, show how the
  different reasons were connected.

2 Soldiers of Britain and the Empire

Preparing for a long war

On the morning of 5 August the British Prime Minister chose his War Minister: Lord Kitchener. He was Britain's best known soldier who had led the armies which had defeated the Boers in South Africa in 1902. That afternoon Kitchener told a meeting of cabinet ministers, generals and admirals:

> **1** *We must be prepared to put armies of millions into the field and maintain them for several years . . . A nation like Germany, after having forced the issue, will not give in until it is beaten to the ground. That will take a very long time. No one living knows how long.*

Lord Kitchener speaking to the War Council, 5 August 1914

At the start of the war, Britain had a small, professional army. It was the only major European country that did not have a large 'conscript' army (which all young men were forced to serve in). The Government said that Kitchener could now build a 'New Army' of volunteers. By the end of 1914, 54 million recruiting posters had been printed. Some 12,000 public meetings were held where army officers, clergymen and well-known local people called on men to volunteer to fight for their country. Many joined 'Pals Battalions' of men who lived in the same town and did the same kind of work.

Who volunteered?

By February 1916 more than three million men had volunteered to join Kitchener's 'New Army'. This was a great number: why did so many men want to join? Did they volunteer out of patriotism? Or did they have other reasons?

1 In August 1914 many people were saying the war would be 'over by Christmas'. How would someone who agreed with Kitchener explain why they were wrong?

2 What else besides soldiers would Britain need if the war became as hard and long as Kitchener believed?

How important was government propaganda in persuading them to join? Did the sort of work a man did have any connection with whether he was likely to volunteer? Look at the sources below:

3 **Imagine a meeting of the artist and the copy-writer (the person who writes the words) who designed the recruiting posters (sources 2–5).**
a) How would they have explained their aims?
b) Is there any evidence from the soldiers (sources 6–9) that the posters worked?

Recruiting posters.

2

3

4

TO THE WOMEN OF BRITAIN.

1. You have read what the Germans have done in Belgium. Have you thought what they would do if they invaded this Country

2. Do you realise that the safety of your home and children depends on our getting more men **NOW**

3. Do you realise that the one word "GO" from you may send another man to fight for our King and Country

4. When the War is over and someone asks your husband or your son what he did in the great War, is he to hang his head because you would not let him go

WON'T YOU HELP AND SEND A MAN TO JOIN THE ARMY TO-DAY?

5

1 **Some women looked out for young men not in uniform to give white feathers, a sign of cowardice.**
  a) Why did it work in the case of H. Symonds (source 9)?
  b) What reasons might other men give for being even more determined *not* to join the army?
2 **Look at source 10. Which groups of workers joined in the biggest proportions? Suggest reasons why they were more eager to go to war.**
3 **What problems would be caused in Britain by having:**
  a) a large army to supply;
  b) men from industry and transport joining the Army?

6 *I offer on behalf of the City of Birmingham to raise and equip a battalion of business men for service in His Majesty's Army, to be called the Birmingham Battalion.*

W. H. Bowater, Deputy Mayor, 1914

7 *I felt that what we were going to do was something that had just got to be done. Had not the Kaiser [Emperor of Germany] invaded Belgium and were not the Germans a bad crowd? Our intention was to defeat them and put them back in their proper place.*

Private Thomas Bickerton, *The Wartime Experiences of an Ordinary Tommy*, 1964

8 *I had just signed articles of clerkship in my father's office, to become a solicitor, and had to face the prospect of going down to the office every morning and coming back from the office every evening for the next five solid years. And here was a glorious opportunity to break away and look for adventure.*

Lieutenant Philip Howe, in M. Brown, *Tommy goes to War*, 1970

9 *I was listening to a ginger-haired girl giving a recruiting speech at Hyde Park Corner on 24 July 1915. I was seventeen at the time but eager to go. So when 'Ginger' gently pushed a white feather into my buttonhole, I went off to the recruiting office.*

H. Symonds, speaking in 1964

10 Volunteers for the New Army.

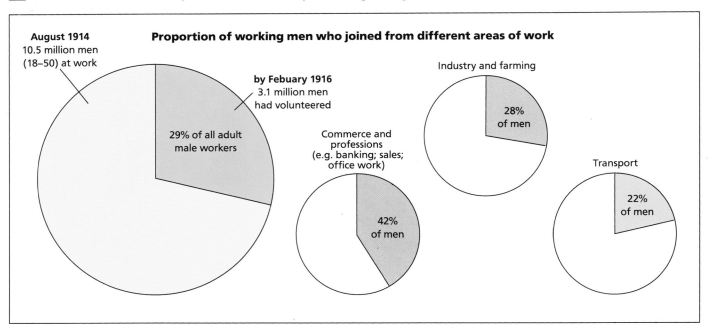

Proportion of working men who joined from different areas of work

August 1914
10.5 million men (18–50) at work

by Febuary 1916
3.1 million men had volunteered

29% of all adult male workers

Commerce and professions (e.g. banking; sales; office work) — 42% of men

Industry and farming — 28% of men

Transport — 22% of men

11 Recruiting poster.

Soldiers of the Empire

There were 450 million people in the British Empire – a quarter of the human race. About 200 million lived in India. In the First World War, about 1¼ million Indian soldiers fought for Britain in Europe or the Middle East. The West Indies, with their tiny population of 2 million, sent 15,000 volunteers.

About 25 million people in the Empire were originally from English, Scots, Welsh and Irish families who had emigrated to countries such as Australia, New Zealand, Canada, and South Africa. Nearly 1½ million of them volunteered to fight for the Empire.

This poem was written by an Australian:

12 *The bugles of England are blowing o'er the sea,*
Calling out over the years, calling now to me.
They woke me from dreaming in the dawning of the day.
The bugles of England; and how could I stay?

J. D. Burns, 1914

The soldiers of the Empire added to the number of men that Britain could send to war. But what mattered most in 1914 was that they would be on their way to the Front in early 1915, months before any of the New Army volunteers were trained. The events of 1914 and the first part of 1915 show how important that was.

The first fighting: France 1914

The Germans advance

In the first weeks of war, the German Army advanced swiftly through Belgium and northern France. Brussels fell to the Germans on 20 August. All was going according to plan for a knock-out blow against France (see page 22).

By 17 August, the British Expeditionary Force (BEF) had arrived in France and 63 aircraft of the Royal Flying Corps (RFC) had flown to join them. By 20 August the British were at Mauberge, guarding the end of the French line, leaving France's two million soldiers free to attack the Germans further south.

Just two days later, British pilots returned with news that they had seen Germans advancing and the French retreating. The British moved into Mons to stop the enemy advance, and found themselves facing the whole German First Army. The British were heavily outnumbered. The only possible move

4 What had J. D. Burns in mind by writing that the bugles were 'calling out over the years' (source 12)?

5 How do these Australian sources (sources 11 and 12) appeal to similar feelings and ideas?

13 The German advance, 1914.

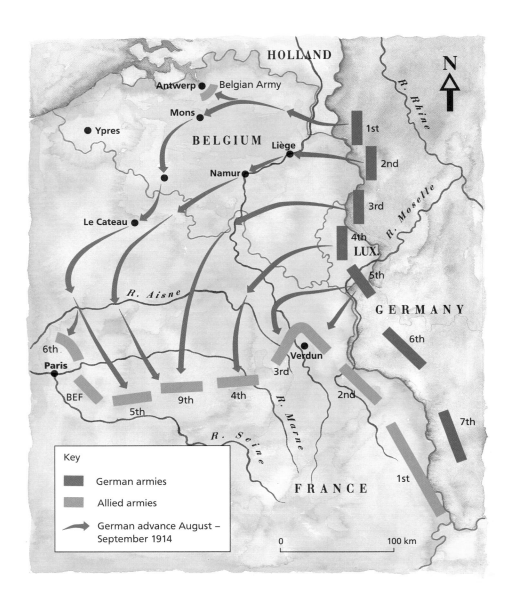

was to fight and then quickly retreat to get out of Mons. Coolness and discipline meant that only 1,800 British soldiers were killed or wounded. A sixteen year-old trumpeter, J. Naylor, watched a BEF rifle company:

14 *And the officer, still as cool as anything, was saying, 'At two-fifty . . . At two hundred . . .' And then he said, 'ten rounds rapid!' and the chaps opened up – and the Germans just fell down like logs. I've never seen anything like it, the discipline, the fire discipline of those troops . . . I thought, 'What a marvellous army we are!'*

Quoted in L. Macdonald, *1914*, 1987

After this escape, the retreat from Mons took the BEF about three hundred kilometres further south, pursued by the Germans. Rifleman E. Gale remembered:

1 What did Naylor mean by 'discipline'? Why should the BEF's discipline be better than the Germans'?

15 *I don't suppose we had more than an hour's sleep at a time in all that ten days. I tell you, us drivers going along the road with the transport got so sick and tired of riding in the saddle that we got off and walked. . . . the infantry; they were in a worse condition than what we were. They had to hoof it all the way, and same as us, if they stopped anywhere they could only get a few minute's sleep.*

Quoted in L. Macdonald, *1914*, 1987

On 26 August, at Le Cateau, the Germans were so close that the BEF had to turn and fight. This time about 8,000 British soldiers were killed or wounded; the rest marched on.

> **2** How does this scene (source 16) agree with the trumpeter's description (source 14)?
> **3** What sort of countryside was the battle fought in?

16 Riflemen face the enemy at the Battle of Le Cateau, 1914.

The miracle of the Marne: counter-attack

Despite some fierce fighting on the way, by 3 September the German Army was fast approaching Paris. The capital seemed about to fall to the Germans. But the German generals made a key mistake. The Schlieffen Plan had laid down that they should sweep around Paris, encircling the British and French. Instead they marched to face them along the River Marne.

The Germans were surprised at the strong counter-attack, mostly by the French. The Allies stopped the enemy advance, dashing the Germans' hope for a swift victory over France. Paris taxi-drivers helped to save their city by shuttling 4,000 soldiers to the Front.

> **4** Explain how the Battle of the Marne meant that the Schlieffen Plan had failed.

A 'slogging match' in Flanders

The French and the BEF pushed the Germans from the Marne to the River Aisne. Then the war of movement stopped. The German line 'dug in' on the high ground north of the river. Drummer E. L. Slaytor remembered the date:

17
Our orders were to advance on the village of Ostel . . . We had gone just a few hundred yards when we came under heavy rifle fire, machine-gun fire and shellfire . . . we were given the order to retire and form a firing line . . .

We got no further, and after a couple of days a line on more or less the same spot was more or less stabilised. We bogged down. And that was that.

That would have been about 16 September.

Quoted in L. Macdonald, *1914*, 1987

That date, 16 September 1914, was six weeks after the outbreak of war. The German Army had moved from Belgium to Paris and part of the way back. Now both sides began to dig two lines of trenches which stretched from the Swiss border to Belgium. Both sides were to occupy much the same positions till the end of the war. The soldiers who were not needed to defend the trenches were moved by train to Flanders, where a war of movement was still possible. The BEF had lost about a quarter of its men but they were joined by Canadian regiments, and some British Territorial, or part-time, soldiers.

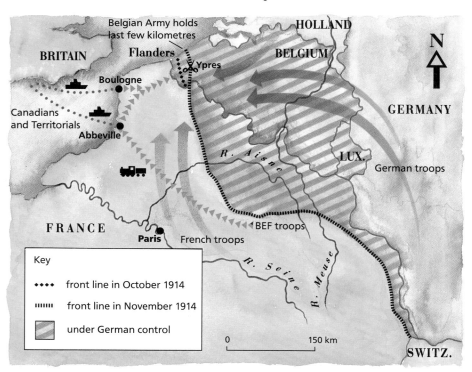

18 Fighting in Flanders, October–November 1914.

1 Compare this photograph
(source 20) with the painting of
Le Cateau (source 16). How
had the nature of fighting
changed? Could anyone have
realised that the war would stay
in the trenches for four years?
2 What had Kitchener said about
the war in August 1914
(source 1)? How does the story
of events in October and
November show that he was
correct?
3 The men who fought with the
BEF in 1914 called themselves
'The Old Contemptibles'. Why
did they choose this name?
(Source 15 on page 17 may give
you a clue.) What evidence
have you seen that the BEF was
not 'contemptible' (worthy of
scorn)?

Flanders is flat and criss-crossed with streams, canals and ditches. If their banks are broken the land can quickly become a quagmire. Each side now 'dug in' to shallow holes or shell craters with a few sandbags in front. They waited for their artillery to shell the enemy's dug-outs and then crept forward with rifles, machine guns and grenades. Sometimes they captured a dug-out, but just as often they were wiped out by enemy machine-gun fire.

The first Battle of Ypres

For the British it was vital to stop the Germans breaking through to the market town of Ypres and on to the Channel ports. The last German assault on Ypres came on 11 November. Corporal Holbrook remembered this event fifty years later:

19 *We were about five hundred strong then. We had about thirty or so officers the night before. By 9 a.m. on 11 November we had 34 men left . . . We lost all our officers, except one . . . I knew where I was facing but there wasn't a soul near me. They had been killed and wounded.*

Quoted in L. Macdonald, *1914*, 1987

After that, the battle 'First Ypres', died out. It was to be the last burst of open warfare on the Western Front. Soldiers were ordered to extend the line of trenches to the Channel coast. A continuous line of battle now stretched about 725 kilometres, from Switzerland to the North Sea.

The First Battle of Ypres cost 58,000 British men killed or wounded. The BEF had set out with 100,000 men. The total losses of the BEF since August were 89,000. As an army it had been virtually wiped out. The future lay with the men in England volunteering to join Kitchener's New Army.

20 Scots Guards in a hastily-dug trench in Flanders.

Disaster in the Dardanelles, 1915

1 Why should the British War
   Council be worried about a
   'slogging match' on the
   Western Front?

2 If the Allies helped Russia and
   Serbia, how might that help
   their armies on the Western
   Front?

3 Why might Greece, Romania
   and Bulgaria join the Allies?

4 What difference would Turkey
   make to the Central Powers'
   chance of victory?

5 'ANZACs' were soldiers serving
   with the Australian and New
   Zealand Army Corps. How
   would the ANZAC forces have
   travelled to Egypt?

The terrible losses at the First Battle of Ypres put a question mark over Britain's war plans. Would Britain have to send an endless stream of young volunteers to die on the Western Front?

So far the Navy had played only a small part in the war. The Minister in charge, Winston Churchill, was itching to find it a job. On 13 January, ministers, generals and admirals gathered for a meeting of the War Council. Lord Hankey describes the meeting:

> **21** *Churchill suddenly revealed his well-kept secret of a naval attack on the Dardanelles! The idea caught on at once . . . The War Council turned eagerly from the dreary vista of a 'slogging match' on the Western Front to brighter prospects, as they seemed, in the Mediterranean. The Navy . . . was to come into the front line.*

Lord Hankey, Secretary of the War Council, in *The Supreme Command*, Vol. 1, 1961

Why the Dardanelles?

The Dardanelles is a narrow strait in north-west Turkey. It was important for the Allies to try to control the waterway, so they could send aid to their ally, Russia. Churchill's plan was to send warships into the Dardanelles to knock out Turkish guns and pull up the mines with nets. Next the British would send

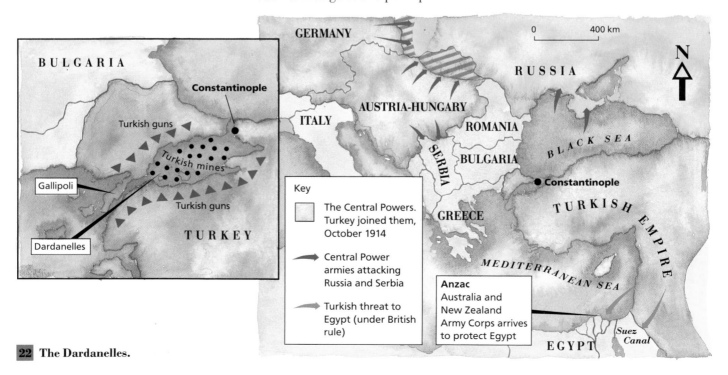

22 The Dardanelles.

troops to capture Constantinople (now called Istanbul). The way would then be open to send supplies to Russia to stiffen its armies against Germany and Austria-Hungary.

On 18 March, 28 battleships tried to force their way through the Dardanelles. Turkish guns and mines sank three cruisers and crippled three others. A total of 700 men died. The British fleet withdrew. What should the British do next?

The Gallipoli campaign, 1915

It was decided that the only way to break through the Dardanelles was to send soldiers across Gallipoli to destroy the Turkish guns and forts. Gallipoli is a narrow and rugged peninsula between the Dardanelles and the Agean Sea, and is about 100 kilometres long. It was to become the scene of a costly and disastrous campaign by the Allies. The Australians and New Zealanders of the ANZAC Army were sent from Egypt. Kitchener sent Britain's last regular army division, the 29th.

On 15 April they landed at Helles and Anzac Cove. The narrow beaches were crowded with soldiers under heavy Turkish gunfire. Both Allied armies were short of maps, water and food, and any means of signalling to each other.

23 The landing at Anzac Cove: an Australian war artist's view. Painting by George Lambert.

6 What do sources 22–24 tell you about the difficulties soldiers faced in the first hours of the landing?

A British officer's account of the landing at Helles:

24 *... One of the men close to me fell back dead – shot ... I jumped out at once into the sea (up to my chest) yelling at the men to make a rush for it and follow me. But the poor devils – packed like sardines in a tin and carrying this damnable weight on their backs – could scarcely clamber over the boat and only two reached the shore un-hit ...*

Major David French, writing to his parents in England

During April and May, the men of ANZAC and the 29th fought their way to rocky ridges above the beaches. By 8 May there were 20,000 dead. Thousands were evacuated with wounds, and even more because of diseases caused by poor food and lack of sanitation.

The poet A. P. Herbert, who served in the 29th Division, described the scene:

> **25**
> *The flies! Oh God, the flies*
> *   That spoiled the sacred dead.*
> *To see them swarm from dead men's eyes*
> *   And share the soldier's bread!*
> *Nor think I now forget*
> *   The filth and stench of war,*
> *The corpses on the parapet*
> *   The maggots in the floor.*

A. P. Herbert, 'Half-hours at Helles', 1916

The arrival of an Indian brigade of Sikhs, Gurkhas and Punjabis, and then a second landing at Suvla Bay, could not overcome the problems of the rough countryside, heat and disease. In December 1915 the whole invasion force evacuated Gallipoli quietly by night without loss of life. Evacuation was the only success of a campaign which cost 49,000 British, ANZAC and Indian lives, and more than 200,000 wounded.

The Dardanelles and Gallipoli campaigns were failures in themselves. But their most important result was that by the end of 1915, the British had failed to find a way of avoiding the long and murderous slog in Belgium and France, which had faced them at the end of 1914.

1 In 1970 the military historian, Corelli Barnett wrote:

The Dardanelles expedition failed even in its immediate objectives because it was neither large enough nor well-enough equipped, trained and organised to fulfill the ambitious strategic vision.

C. Barnett, *Britain and her Army*, 1970

With the help of Lord Hankey's memoirs (source 21) and the map (source 22), explain what the 'strategic vision was'.

2 **With the help of the map (source 22), explain what the 'immediate objectives' were.**

3 **Why does Corelli Barnett suggest that the expedition failed?**

4 **Suppose that Britain and France had sent a million men with equipment, rather than half a million. What effect might that have had on the war in France?**

Review and Assessment

1 Look at sources 2–10 (on pages 19 to 20).

  a How can these sources be used to show an important difference between Britain's Army and those elsewhere in Europe?

  b Was it easy or difficult to persuade men to volunteer in 1914? Use the evidence to support your answer.

  c In which ways is the diagram in source 10 (i) more useful (ii) less useful than the recruiting posters and the soldiers' accounts?

2 In the section on the Dardanelles (pages 26–28) there is a painting (source 23), a letter (source 24), and a poem (source 25).

  a Discuss how each source helps you to understand what it was like to be a soldier on Gallipoli.

  b Which source do you think gives the most powerful impression – and why?

  c If you had to choose the one which was closest to the truth about the campaign which would it be? Why?

3 Compare the poems on page 21 (source 12) and 28 (source 25).
Explain how each could be useful to a historian trying to write about the British Army in 1914–15.

4 Apart from the letter about Gallipoli (source 24), all the quotations from soldiers in this chapter were written down about fifty years later. In which ways would they be (i) less valuable and (ii) more valuable as evidence than those written down shortly after the event?

3 The Western Front: men and arms

Trench warfare

From early 1915 the two sides faced each other in France across the No Man's Land which lay between their lines of trenches. Each side's trenches marked the front line of a war zone which stretched back eastwards into Germany or westwards through France and into Britain. As the war progressed the British Army took over many extra kilometres of trench from the French. As they did so, the number of British men and women behind the front line increased.

In 1914 there were 13 million men aged between 15 and 45 in Britain. About 4.5 million of them served on the Western Front during the First World War, as well as several thousand British women and about a million men from the British Empire. About half a million never returned.

1 Look at the cross-section (source 1A). What do you think the following are for:
   a) duckboards; b) fire step; c) parapet; d) parados?

2 Refer to the diagram (source 1B). How far apart are the two front lines? How many different kinds of trenches are there?

3 Suggest three ways that the enemy could be held up if they broke through No Man's Land.

1 The trench system.

A cross-section of a fire trench

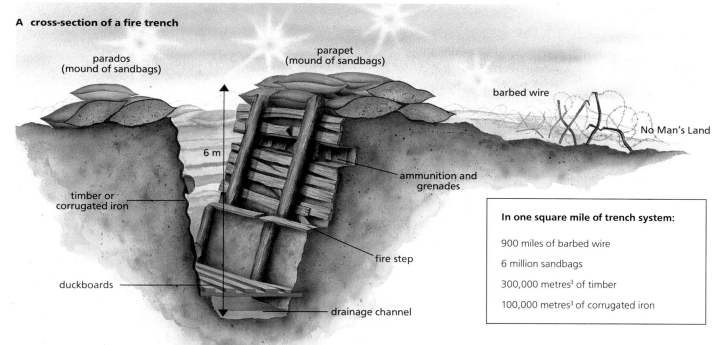

parados
(mound of sandbags)

parapet
(mound of sandbags)

barbed wire

No Man's Land

6 m

ammunition and
grenades

timber or
corrugated iron

fire step

duckboards

drainage channel

In one square mile of trench system:

900 miles of barbed wire

6 million sandbags

300,000 metres^3 of timber

100,000 metres^3 of corrugated iron

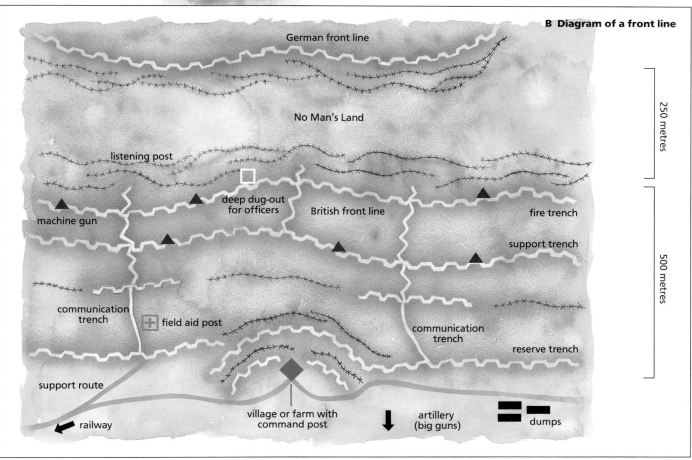

B Diagram of a front line

German front line

No Man's Land

250 metres

listening post

deep dug-out
for officers

British front line

fire trench

machine gun

support trench

500 metres

communication
trench

field aid post

communication
trench

reserve trench

support route

railway

village or farm with
command post

artillery
(big guns)

dumps

1 How many different kinds of
   transport are shown in the
   photograph (source 3)?
2 How does the picture suggest
   the limitations of motor
   vehicles at the time?
3 What problems would there be
   in evacuating wounded
   soldiers?

Supplies to the Front

The soldiers at the Front needed food, ammunition, barbed wire, shells, timber, sandbags. Every gun team needed oats to feed six horses. The supplies came by train to depots just a few kilometres behind the trenches. The front-line soldiers then moved the supplies to the trenches at night, under enemy shellfire. How did they transport them?

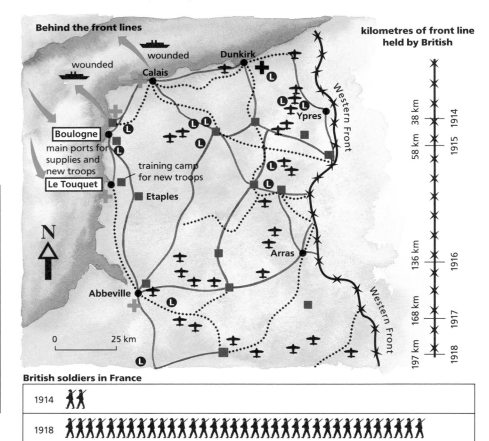

Key

■	depots, bases
✚	hospitals (90,000 beds; 20,000 doctors; 114,000 orderlies; 6,000 nurses)
✈	aerodromes
ⓛ	Chinese labourers' camps
.....	railways used by British army
—	roads
Boulogne	main port for supplies and new troops

2 Behind the front line.

British soldiers in France

| 1914 | 🚶🚶 |
| 1918 | 🚶🚶🚶🚶🚶🚶🚶🚶🚶🚶🚶🚶🚶🚶🚶🚶🚶🚶🚶🚶🚶🚶🚶🚶🚶 |

100,000   500,000   1,000,000   1,500,000

3 Soldiers moving shells to the front line.

By 1918 the British Army had 37,000 lorries, but they had to keep to proper roads. The ground near the trenches was often boggy, and there was nothing like the modern Landrover to travel cross-country. That was a job for horses. In 1918 the Army had 400,000 horses, but horses were slow in muddy ground. So thousands of kilometres of light railway were laid. Lorry engines were then fitted with wheels to run on the rails.

Life in the trenches

Soldiers were lucky if the trenches were like those in the diagram (source 1). In wet places the sides of the trenches were never firm, and thick black mud came up through the duckboards.

Life in the trenches was extremely grim; the risk to life constant. Surprisingly, during the first winter, the soldiers' health and morale remained fairly high. One of the most common complaints, though, was 'trenchfoot'. This was caused by exposing feet to cold water for too long. Feet could turn blue or red, a mass of severe chilblains. In extreme cases, gangrene could set in. Foot inspections were part of everyday life for the soldiers.

Another common problem in the trenches was lice. Men had to live close together, wearing the same clothes for days on end. Naturally, lice spread rapidly in these conditions. Bath houses were set up behind the front line where men coming out of the trenches could have a hot bath and a complete change of clothes. As well as itching and discomfort, lice caused a more serious problem: 'trench fever'. Its symptoms were similar to flu and typhoid, and many soldiers suffered from its effects.

4 **Write a paragraph or use a diagram to explain:**
a) **the part that Britain expected to play in the European War in 1914;**
b) **how this had changed by 1917–18;**
c) **how this was likely to effect industry in Britain.**
5 **How would the change affect Germany?**

4 **An advertisement for a remedy for parasites.**

Soldiers usually spent a few days at a time in the trenches, followed by a few in a rest camp. The busiest time was at night when parties went into No Man's Land to repair barbed wire, bring in wounded soldiers, or to lob grenades into German trenches. During the day there might be little to do and boredom could set in. But sometimes the time might be spent like this:

5 *During these four days Fritz* [the Germans] *shelled with 5.9 guns. Down I would get to the bottom of the trench and almost try to burrow in like a rabbit, as the big shell came screaming down at us, the explosion making my trousers stick to my legs for a moment, and the feeling of relief as the shell burst a safe distance away, the pieces flying all directions, humming their different tunes.*

George Ashurst, *My Bit*, 1987

The heavy shelling and gas attacks made life in the trenches even more unpleasant. One soldier describes the scene in the winter of 1917:

6 *As far as the eye could see was a mass of black mud with shell holes filled with water. Here and there broken duckboards, partly submerged in the quagmire; here and there a horse's carcass sticking out of the water; here and there a corpse. The only sign of life was a rat or two swimming about to find food and a patch of ground.*

    At night a yellow mist hung over the mud; the stench was almost unbearable. When gas shells came over the mist turned to brown. It smelt like violets. The smell of violets was a sign of danger.

Private H. Jeary, in L. Macdonald, *1914–18*, 1988

However, the troops tried to keep their spirits up, particularly at special times. An army chaplain describes Christmas at the Front in 1917:

7 *Although the battalion was in the line, we determined to see that Christmas was properly observed . . . I made friends with the cook, and together we drew up the menu and produced the following remarkable effusion:*

XMAS DAY MENU

SOUPE MAÎTRE DE DUGOUT
POISSON PILCHARD DANS LA BOÎTE
BULLE AU BOEUF
POUDING NOËL

The King   Absent friends

The Revd S. Hinchcliffe, in L. Macdonald, *1914–18*, 1988

1 **Look at source 8. List the branches of the British Forces which: a) grew; b) shrank in importance during the war.**
2 **In which ways did the following become more specialised: a) infantry; b) the Air Force; c) non-combatants (non-fighters)? Why do you think cavalrymen often transferred from horses to tanks?**
3 **Explain how the changes in the Army were linked to changes from a war of movement to one of trench-fighting.**
4 **What effect would these changes have on industry in Britain?**

New ways of killing

Up to 1915, generals had trained their troops for wars of *movement*. Field guns would tear holes in enemy lines; infantry would then move forward to capture the weakened position; while cavalry dashed through the gap.

Nothing like that was now possible. For all of the period 1915–17, the main battles lasted for weeks or months. They involved hundreds of thousands of men backed up by new and more powerful weapons. It became a war of *attrition*, or wearing down. The most important thing seemed to be to kill or wound vast numbers of the enemy and destroy their equipment. New weapons of destruction were constantly needed, and they in turn needed men with more specialist skills to operate, repair and move them. As we shall see in Chapter 4, the new weapons also made heavy demands on workers, both men and women, back in Britain.

8 The British Army in France in 1914 and 1918. How did it change?

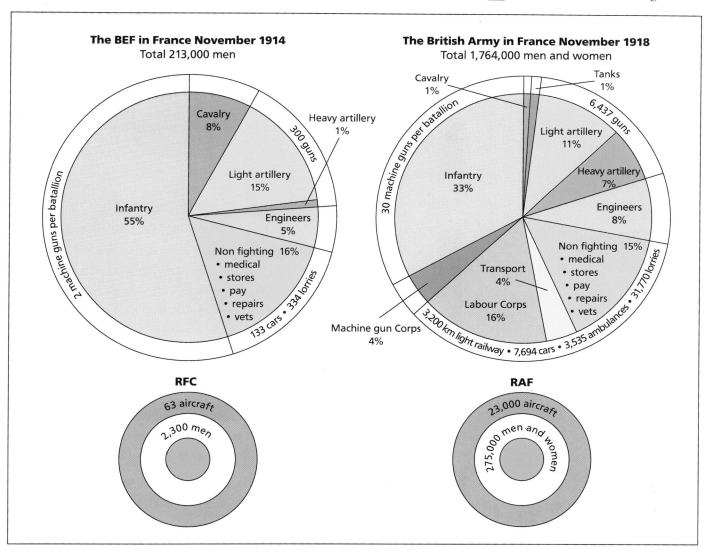

From horseback to tank

The problem of using horses in battle:

9 German machine gunners in a trench.

As an American officer explained:

10 *You can't have a cavalry charge until you have captured the enemy's last machine gun.*

Unknown

A British colonel at the Somme describes a cavalry attack:

11 *I descried* [could just see] *a squadron of Indian cavalry, dark faces under glistening helmets, galloping across the valley towards the slope . . . these masters of horsemanship galloped through a hell of fire, lifting their mounts lightly over yawning shell-holes; turning and twisting through the barrage of great shells; the ranks thinned, not a man escaped.*

Lt-Col. G. Seton Hutchinson, *Warrior*, 1932

1 Cavalry had played a leading part in wars for two thousand years. How did the technology of 1914–15 affect the usefulness of horsemen?

2 Generals still tried to use cavalry at the Battle of the Somme and even in later battles. What job were they hoping the cavalry would do?

The solution:

12 *. . . a power-driven, bullet-proof, armed engine capable of destroying machine-guns, of crossing country and trenches, of breaking through entanglements and of climbing earthworks.*

Colonel Swinton of the Royal Engineers, November 1914

Army and Navy engineers worked on Colonel Swinton's idea. They code-named it 'tank' so the enemy would believe they were making a water-carrier! On 29 January 1916, a 'Mark 1', tank was tested on a mock battlefield. General Douglas Haig ordered the new weapons for the Army in France. In two battles he used them after shelling had turned the ground into a swamp. There were some 'teething troubles', though. At Passchendaele in 1917:

13 *Most of the day's history for tank commanders could be summed up in the fateful words, 'Bellied in boggy ground' . . . The majority sank lower and lower, until the water came in through the sponson doors and stopped the engines.*

Lt. F. Mitchell, *I was There*, 1918

The first battle to *start* with a tank attack was Cambrai in 1917. A total of 378 tanks moved forward, with the infantry walking in files behind. About seven kilometres of enemy ground was captured. The advance ended because 65 tanks had been destroyed by German shells, 71 had broken down and 43 got stuck in ditches.

3 Explain why tanks were:
   a) rhomboid in shape; b) had caterpillar tracks instead of wheels.
4 Explain the difference between the way tanks were used at Passchendaele and at Cambrai.
5 Was the tank a complete or part solution to the problem of attacking trenches? Explain your answer.

14 A Mark V tank breaking down barbed wire in 1918.

After Cambrai, Britain and France started large-scale production of tanks. The British made 2,818, and the French more than 4,000. The Germans made only 20. Their generals thought that anti-tank guns were more important. By the summer of 1918 tanks had at last improved in reliability and speed. They played an important part in the final defeat of Germany's forces.

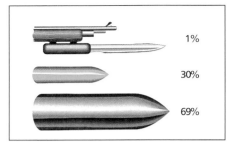

1%
30%
69%

15 Causes of wounds to soldiers.

1 **What does this diagram (source 15) tell you about the nature of fighting in the Great War?**

2 **What is Paul Nash's view of the 'new world' (source 17)?**
3 **How can the picture be used to explain the effects of heavy shelling like that on the Somme and at Passchendaele?**
4 **What difficulties would shelling make for infantrymen who had to fight over this ground?**
5 **Compare this with the photograph of Passchendaele on page 79 (source 10).**
   a) Has Paul Nash exaggerated?
   b) Which picture do you think gives the most vivid picture of the effects of shelling?
6 **The title of source 17 is an example of *irony*? What does this mean?**

Machine guns and shelling

Machine guns were used widely and effectively during the war. They were the great weapon of defence. Every rifleman had a bayonet – a sharp blade that could be attached to the end of their rifle – but if they tried a bayonet charge, they were quickly mown down by bullets from the rapid-firing machine gun. During the war, infantry were given more machine guns. In 1914 there was one machine gun to 150 men; by 1918 it was one to ten.

In 1914 nearly all the BEF's 300 artillery were light field guns which fired shrapnel. But shrapnel did little damage to men in trenches: it was more effective in battle on open ground. So in 1915, Britain began a massive effort to make heavy guns and high explosive shells. In 1916 and 1917, battles now began with days of heavy artillery bombardment before the infantry attack, and the shelling increased in frightfulness.

16 How much shelling?

Battle	Length of front	Number of heavy guns	Number of shells
Somme 1916	25 km	1,437	3.00 million
Passchendaele 1917	25 km	3,091	4.25 million

17 A war artist's view of the results of heavy shelling. 'We are making a new world', painting by Paul Nash, 1918.

Gas – the chemists' war

In April 1915 the Germans started the Second Battle of Ypres. In their trenches were 6,000 metal canisters filled with compressed liquid chlorine. On 22 April, the wind blew towards the Allies. German soldiers turned the taps on the canisters and a yellow-green cloud rolled over No Man's Land, followed by German infantry wearing gas masks. The first victims of the gas attack were French North Africans. Two days later it was the turn of Canadians and Indians. An army chaplain rode out to them, and described the horrific scene:

18 *We found men lying all along the road gasping out their lives, and with sinking hearts we recognised the deadly effects of the German gas. At 8.30 the death-cloud had swept down upon them, the men had not been able to face it . . . They had run gasping until they fell black in the face and dying . . .*

Revd O. S. Watkins, in W. Moore, *Gas Attack*, 1987

About 6,000 soldiers died from gas poisoning. If the Germans had had more men they might have won the Second Battle of Ypres. All they did, though, was to convince the Allies that their armies must have gas too. A team of scientists set to work in Britain. Five months later, in September 1915, the British used chlorine at the Battle of Loos. The Germans lost over a kilometre of land before they were able to fight back.

Methods of attacking with gas improved. Instead of letting off containers of gas, each side soon started to fire gas in shells from long-range guns, so that wind direction no longer mattered. By 1918 one in four shells was gas-filled. New forms of gas were made, too. As well as chlorine there was phosgene and later mustard gas. All had terrible effects. Mustard gas was first used by the Germans in July 1917. The yellow gas was the most widely used by the end of the war, and its effects were very unpleasant. Men were blinded. Huge yellow blisters appeared on any exposed skin. Lungs were stripped of their linings.

7 There was a lot of argument at the time about whether it was right to use gas in battle. How could this picture (source 19) be used to support arguments a) for and b) against?

19 Soldiers blinded by gas. Painting by John Singer, about 1918.

The Air Force – the Army's eyes

Before the war, no one was sure how useful aeroplanes would really be in the fighting. In 1912 the British Army started the Royal Flying Corps. From the air, airmen could survey great areas and then report back quickly. Aircraft soon proved to be vital for observing enemy movements and finding targets for the artillery. It was pilots of the RFC and French Air Service, for example, who spotted that the German Army had changed direction towards Paris, which led to the crucial Battle of the Marne in 1914.

Each RFC plane had a pilot and an observer with a notebook and map strapped to his knees. They had instructions like this:

> **20** *Don't forget to use your field-glasses on the rolling-stock* [locomotives on railways]; *don't forget the precise direction of trains and motor transport; don't forget the roads and railways on every side; don't forget the canals.*
>
> Alan Bolt, *Contact: An Airman's Outings*, 1916

1 Why was such information important?

In 1915 cameras were fitted so that observers could take aerial photographs. On the ground this forced troops to use camouflage paint. Soon aircraft were fitted with wireless so that observers could tap out messages in morse code.

There were two main ways of stopping the airmen's information getting back. One was the anti-aircraft gun. The other was the single-seater fighter plane.

The years of 1915 and 1916 were the time of the 'ace' fighter pilots who twisted and turned their aircraft to get an enemy in their sights for a machine-gun blast. From the ground these struggles looked like 'dog-fights'. Their exploits captured the public imagination. But it was not a sport. Pilots faced almost certain death in a matter of months. One survivor noted in his diary:

> **21** *Had a terrible nightmare last night. Jumped out of my bed eleven times even though I tried to stop myself by tying my pyjama strings to the bed . . . It was the usual old business of being shot down in flames and jumping out of my aeroplane.*
>
> Ira Jones, *An Airfighter's Scrapbook*, 1938

From 1917 onwards, the age of the aces and solo fights were over. British fighters now went up in squadrons so that they could protect each other. By

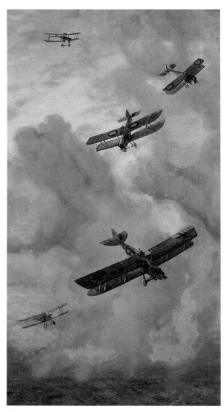

22 Air warfare. 'Putting out his Eyes', a painting by George Horace Davis, 1919.

2 Which two kinds of aircraft can you see here (source 22)?

3 Is 'Putting out his Eyes' a good title? How does it link with what Ira Jones says about fighters in source 21?

4 What would happen if bullets hit the petrol tank of one of these planes?

then, too, aeroplanes were used increasingly for bombing. Although not terribly accurate in bombing raids, aircraft were fitted with improved bomb-sights (a device for aiming bombs), and could attack German bases well behind the trenches.

The Germans had used Zeppelin airships for bombing civilian targets from the start of the war. By 1916 the Zeppelins were replaced by twin-engine Gotha aeroplanes. In May 1917 for example, they bombed Folkestone, causing considerable damage and loss of lives. In 1918 British bombers also made regular raids on cities inside Germany. Although there was nothing like the scale of bombing that was to be seen in the Second World War, a new dimension had now been added to war: air bombardment.

5 In April 1918 the RFC became the Royal Air Force. What changes had earned its new position as the third armed force alongside the Navy and Army?

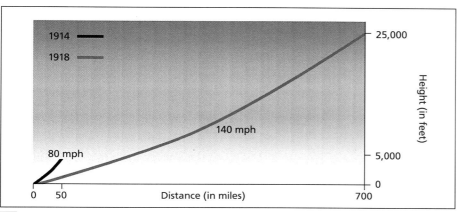

23 **How well did aircraft fly?**

Non-combatants

There were many people directly involved in the war effort, who did not actually fight. These 'non-combatants' played a crucial role. They included doctors, nurses, drivers, cooks and office clerks, both behind the front line and providing support from the home country.

To keep the industrialised war going, extra workers were urgently needed in army repair workshops and stores, at ports and on railways. Thousands of clerks were also needed. If soldiers did these jobs there would be too few fighting at the Front. So their place was taken by special labour and transport units. At first these units were filled with workers from Britain, but soon, they too, were called to the fighting. Overseas labourers were then recruited to fill the places. Their pay and living conditions were far poorer than those of soldiers.

24 **Overseas labourers in France**

Chinese	96,000
Indian	41,000
South African	18,000
Egyptian	15,000
West Indian	about 1,000

25 A WAAC camp at Abbeville bombed by the Germans, 1918.

26 A WAAC recruiting poster. The aim of the WAAC was to send women to replace men in army camps at home and abroad.

The shortage of men led to a change which would have been unthinkable in 1914. In February 1917, women's branches of the Army, Navy and Air Force were set up. Some 8,000 members of the Women's Auxiliary Army Corps (WAAC) served in France as cooks, ambulance drivers, mechanics, typists and clerks during the war.

Medical services at the Front

On a quiet day about 300 soldiers were wounded on the Western Front. In a battle the numbers could rise to tens of thousands. A soldier wounded in No Man's Land would have to wait until night time for men from his trench to carry him back safely to the Aid Post (see source 1, page 31). Medical Corps stretcher-bearers would then carry him to the Dressing Station.

Doctors at Dressing Stations could do little more than put on bandages or splints, and give morphine (a drug extracted from opium) to men in great pain. The wounded then went by ambulance – often horse-drawn – to a Casualty Clearing Station next to a railway.

Here, the wounded were divided into three groups. The less severely wounded were put on trains and sent to a base hospital. (The luckiest among them were sent straight back to England. They had got a 'Blighty' – a wound which was not severe, but bad enough to take them home.) The second group

1 How does this photograph (source 25) show that by 1918 the trenches were not the only area where lives were at risk?

27 A battlefield Dressing Station.

needed life-saving operations in the Clearing Station. Blood-soaked doctors worked for long hours, amputating badly-damaged limbs, sewing up wounds, and cleaning out the bacteria which might cause the deadly gangrene. The third group went into the 'moribund ward' for those about to die. Nothing could be done but to make their last few hours of life as comfortable as possible.

As well as doctors, around 500 women nurses went to France in 1914. By 1918 there were over 17,000. Just under half were the Army's own trained nurses – or Queen Mary Auxiliaries. The rest were unpaid volunteers, either from the Red Cross or from Volunteer Aid Detachments. Sixty years later a VAD remembered her dread of night duty:

2 How near the front line is this Dressing Station (source 27)?

3 The injured are divided into the walking-wounded and stretcher cases. Find each group.

4 What kinds of treatment would be possible here?

5 Where are the supplies of bandages and splints?

28 He [a wounded soldier] *opened his eyes and said, 'You've been an angel to me.' It made me feel absolutely dreadful. I thought, 'Thank goodness he doesn't know what I've been thinking, just hoping all the time that he wouldn't die when I was on duty.' But he died that night. The night Superintendant came in. She was an elderly Scotswoman and very kind. She said, 'I'll do the laying out and you hold the lantern for me' . . . Half-way through, as we turned the body over, Sister looked at me and shook her head. 'We do have to do some things, don't we!' she said.*

Kitty Kenyon, a VAD, quoted in L. Macdonald, *The Roses of No Man's Land*, 1980

Review and Assessment

1   The Great War was the first war when lorries and tanks were used. Does that mean that generals were stupid to keep cavalry on stand-by right through the war? Explain your answer.

2   It is 1919 and you are a senior army officer. Write some notes for a lecture you are going to give. Your subject is: 'What Britain must do to be ready to fight the next war'. You will refer a lot to the changes which took place during the Great War.

3   Look at the painting (source 17) on page 38, and read this part of a letter that the artist Paul Nash wrote to his wife in November 1917.

> **29** *The rain drives on, the stinking mud becomes more evilly yellow, the shell-holes fill up with green-white water, the roads and tracks are covered in inches of slime, the black dying trees ooze and sweat and the shells never cease. They alone plunge overhead, tearing away the rotting tree stumps, breaking the plank roads, striking down horses and mules, annihilating, maiming, maddening, they lunge into the grave which is this land . . .*
>
> *It is unspeakable, godless, hopeless. I am no longer an artist interested and curious. I am a messenger who will bring back word from the men who are fighting, to those who want the war to go on for ever.*
>
> P. Nash, *An Autobiography and other writings*, 1949

a What does Paul Nash mean by saying that, 'I am no longer an artist . . . I am a messenger'?

b In which ways do you think the painting serves as a 'message'?

c Explain how the painting could be used as evidence for changes (i) in the fighting and (ii) in people's ideas and feelings about the war?

The Home Front

War and industry

Need for shells

LIMITED SUPPLIES THE CAUSE

BRITISH ATTACK CHECKED

The Times, 14 May 1915

This newspaper article goes on to describe how a British shelling of German trenches failed to wipe out the enemy defences. German machine-gunners responded, causing 11,500 British casualties on the first day.

The Government was blamed for not planning for an *industrialised* war. It took two months to make 100,000 shells which the Army could fire in just one day. The urgent shortage of shells forced the Liberal Prime Minister, Herbert Asquith, to form a coalition government with Conservatives and one Labour Minister. Asquith also set up a new government department – the Ministry of Munitions (equipment for war). He put David Lloyd George in charge.

Up to then, the Government had never interfered in industry, except over health and safety. In July 1915 the Munitions of War Act gave Lloyd George powers which no minister had ever held before. His Ministry could now take control of factories belonging to private companies. It could also set up its own 'National Factories' to produce munitions for war.

1 'Capital' (in source 1) refers to the factory owners and shareholders. What is the cartoonist's view of the changes that Lloyd George would bring to war industry?

DELIVERING THE GOODS.

1 'The man of "push and go" takes command of munitions.' Cartoon of Lloyd George, the Minister of Munitions, in *Punch*, 1915.

1 Look carefully at the photograph (source 2). How are the workers protected for work?

Controlled and National Factories

More than 20,000 private factories were 'controlled' during the war. One of the largest Controlled Factories was Herbert Austin's car factory at Longbridge on the outskirts of Birmingham. In 1913 he had 2,000 workers making 80 cars a week. Under government control, new workshops were built for 20,000 workers, both men and women. By the end of the war they had made 9 million shells, 650 artillery guns, 2,000 aeroplanes, 2,500 aero-engines, 480 armoured cars and 2,000 lorries.

Not all Controlled Factories made metal goods. Cadbury's part in the war effort, for example, was to open a Controlled Factory for drying vegetables, and another one for making condensed milk – which both went to men in the trenches.

By 1918 there were 250 National Factories too. Many were for shell-filling. Most workers in these factories were women who mixed chemicals and poured them into shell cases. About 200 women workers were killed by explosions. Other National Factories were safer, though. Tottenham Hotspur football ground, for example, was covered in and fitted out with sewing machines for 1,000 women to make gas masks.

2 Filling shells at a National Factory in Nottinghamshire.

2 In which ways do Sources 2 and 3 agree?

3 Suggest reasons why women might have chosen to work in these factories.

4 What do you think would happen to National Factories and their workers after the war?

In Yorkshire, a group of women asked to see round a National Factory before starting work. This is an account of what they saw:

3 *The workers wore rubber gloves, mob caps, respirators, and leggings. Their faces were coated with flour and starch, to protect them from TNT dust* [trinitrotoluene – a poisonous substance used to make explosives]. *Yet in spite of these precautions their skin was yellow. They asked the manager whether the work was dangerous. He answered: 'Not so very dangerous'. They questioned the women workers, but they whispered they dare not speak of their conditions . . . A few days later the factory was blown up. Thirty-nine people, including the manager, were killed.*

E. Sylvia Pankhurst, *The Home Front*, 1932

4 **Munitions production 1914–18**

Weapons	1914	1915	1916	1917	1918
Guns	91	339	4,314	5,317	8,039
Tanks	—	—	150	1,110	1,359
Machine guns (in thousands)	0.3	6.1	33.5	79.7	120.9
Aero-engines (in thousands)	0.1	1.7	8.4	11.8	22.1
Rifles (in millions)	0.1	0.6	1.0	1.2	1.1
Shells (in millions)	0.5	6.0	45.7	76.2	67.3

5 Which year saw the biggest leap up in production from the previous year (source 4)? How do you account for the change?

6 Which parts of shells were usually made in Controlled Factories? Which parts were made in National Factories?

7 Using source 4, calculate how many shells per day the artillery could fire in 1915, 1916, and 1917.

8 Compare the growth in production of machine guns and rifles (source 4). Describe the differences. What changes did this lead to for the infantry?

9 Why were more aero-engines produced than aircraft?

10 Would the makers of these weapons have learned anything which would help the country *after* the war? Explain your answer.

Women and the war effort

One of the most dramatic changes during the war was in the role of women. Women of all backgrounds played an important part in the war effort. For the first time, many women worked in transport and industry – types of work which had been considered 'unsuitable' for women before the war. Others volunteered for nursing, the Armed Forces and working on the land.

Women's work at the outbreak of war

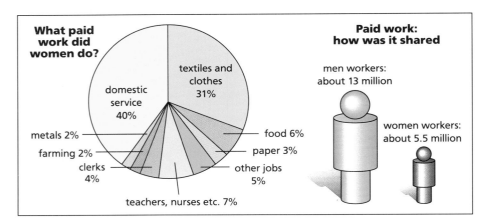

5 Information from the 1911 census.

Compared with today, the range of jobs and careers open to women was extremely narrow in the years just before the Great War. A woman could always find a job as a household servant, or using a sewing machine in a workshop. In Yorkshire or Lancashire she could work in a factory, minding the spinning or weaving machines. But there were many areas of work that were not open to women. There were tens of thousands of buses and trams, for example, but not one female conductor. Smart shops in towns often had only men assistants. No banks had female staff; and many firms had all-male offices. The only careers for which women could train were teaching and nursing.

When war started, many middle-class women joined voluntary groups to knit socks and mittens for soldiers. Some joined Volunteer Aid Detachments as nurses or ambulance drivers. But these were women who could afford not to be paid. The need for women in industry was not seen until the trench-fighting began in earnest in 1915.

By the end of 1915 about $2\frac{1}{4}$ million men had joined the Army. Two million more were needed, but volunteering was slowing down. Recruiting sergeants reported that many men were saying, 'I'll wait until I'm fetched.' At the same time, employers were trying hard to hold on to workers.

Gradually politicians came to agree that Britain must copy the other European countries and have *conscription*. This meant compulsory military

1 Which was the largest area of paid work for women in 1911?
2 Which of the jobs in the pie chart are done by a) far more and b) far fewer women today?

3 Why did posters recruiting women for industry (source 6) replace those recruiting men in 1916?
4 In what ways does this poster have a similar style to the recruiting posters (sources 2–5) on page 19?

6 A recruiting poster, 1916.

service for men. In January 1916, Parliament passed a law to conscript all single men. In March it widened this to include *all* men, single or married, aged 18 to 41. This meant that more women would be needed to replace men in the work-place.

The call for many hands

Women soon began to replace men in transport and office work, as well as in factories. In February 1916, London's largest tram and bus company took on its first women conductors. By 1917 women conductors and ticket collectors were a common sight; so were women driving horse-drawn and electric trams or cleaning buses, trains and station rooms.

In 1914, the War Office had just 25 male clerks for ordering its supplies. By 1918 the Ministry of Munitions had 65,000 men and women. Factories, banks and insurance companies all had to take on women office staff as men joined the Army.

By 1918, over 900,000 women were working in munitions factories too, making shells, guns and aircraft. Most had worked before the war, but they often welcomed the chance to work in factories where pay was higher than in old areas of work, such as domestic service.

Look carefully at the table (source 7).

5 In which areas of work did the number of working women increase or decrease? Complete the 'plus and minus' column.

6 Which four types of work increased most during the war?

7 Which three types of work decreased and why?

8 Which types of new work do you think the women who left their 1914 jobs would go to? Explain your answer.

9 If all the women who left their old jobs moved to new work, how many took a job for the first time? Which work would they be most likely to go to?

7 Changes in women's work 1914–18

Area of work	Number of women employed		
	1914	**1918**	**+ / −**
Munitions (equipment for war)	212,000	947,000	
Textiles	863,000	818,000	
Clothing	612,000	556,000	
Other industries	452,000	451,000	
Transport	18,000	117,000	
Agriculture	190,000	228,000	
Commerce	505,000	934,000	
Self-employed	430,000	470,000	
Hotels, theatres	181,000	220,000	
Professional	542,000	652,000	
Domestic service	1,658,000	1,250,000	
Local and national government (including teaching)	262,000	460,000	
Totals	**5,925,000**	**7,103,000**	

'Dilution' of skills

Before July 1915, millions of jobs in engineering, chemicals and ship-building were kept for skilled men who had served an apprenticeship. But a quarter of all the country's chemical workers and a fifth of all metal-workers and engineers had volunteered for Kitchener's New Army. Under 'dilution', the unions agreed that the jobs could be done by *unskilled* workers until the war ended. The biggest pool of unskilled workers was women.

8 Women turning shells in a Vicker's arms factory, 1917.

1 The women in source 8 are using lathes to shape the nose-cones for large shells. Who would have done this job in 1914?

2 What does 'dilution' mean in everyday language? How does this photograph show dilution in work skills?

Attitudes to women's war work

One woman wrote down these memories of her wartime work:

9 *I was in domestic service and 'hated every minute of it' when war broke out, earning £2 a month working from 6.00 a.m. to 9.00 p.m. So when the need came for women 'war workers' my chance came to 'out'.*

> *I started on hand-cutting shell fuses . . . We worked twelve hours a day apart from the journey morning and night . . . I thought I was very well off earning £5 a week . . .*
>
> *I left . . . in 1916 for a much cleaner and lighter job at the 'Wireless' Teddington where they made the wireless boxes for the signallers in the communications lines in France . . . no doubt the same as my husband was using as he gained his MM [Military Medal].*

Mrs H. A. Felstead, Imperial War Museum, 1976

In 1976 Robert Roberts remembered the war work of his sister, Jane, and her friends:

10 *Having long left the weaving shed, Jane was doing very well for herself turning out shell cases on a capstan lathe at a large new engineering shop. One evening she brought home two jolly country lasses . . . Both girls, previously servants in a great Cheshire house, had been directed into 'munitions' . . . 'What a life!' they said. 'Money to burn!' 'Lovely girls to work with, and fellers!'*

R. Roberts, *A Ragged Schooling*, 1976

3 What reasons does Mrs Felstead give for a) her first change of job and b) her second change?

4 How does the first change of job support information in the table (source 7)?

5 How might you explain the second change from information in Chapter 3 about changes in technology used at the Front?

6 How does this story (source 10) illustrate the information in the table (source 7)?

7 Do you think Jane would be able to keep her job after the war? Explain your answer.

8 Apart from pay, why do you think that Mrs Felstead (in source 9) and Jane's two friends (in source 10) might prefer factory work to domestic service?

Mrs Playne describes some munitions workers she saw at the end of the day:

11 *A short local train came in and disgorged [let out] a couple of hundred de-humanised females . . . judging by the set of their faces bereft of [altogether without] all charm of appearance, clothed anyhow, skin stained yellow-brown even to the roots of their dishevelled hair.*

C. Playne, *A Society at War 1914–16*, 1931

9 Why were the women's skin 'stained yellow-brown'?

10 How does this description (source 11) give a different impression from the other two accounts (sources 9 and 10)?

11 What was likely to be the difference between the jobs done by the women in sources 9 and 10 compared with those in 11?

52

A newspaper described changes in London:

1 Where would the 'business girl' described in source 12 come on the table (source 7)?

12 *The wartime business girl is to be seen dining out alone or with a friend in the moderate-priced restaurants in London. Formerly she would never have had her evening meal in town unless in the company of a man friend. But now with money and without men she is more and more beginning to dine out.*

Daily Mail, September 1915

Technology: old and new

By the middle of 1916, firms and their workers all over the country had stopped making their traditional products. This is a description of Birmingham during the war, but a similar story could have been told about almost any other town or city.

13 *Jewellers abandoned their craftsmanship and the fashioning of gold and silver ornaments for the production of anti-gas apparatus and other war material; old-fashioned firms noted for their art productions . . . turned to the manufacture of an intricate kind of hand grenade. Cycle-makers turned their activities to fuses and shells; world famous pen-makers adapted their machines to the manufacture of cartridge clips; and railway carriage companies launched out with artillery, wagons, limbers [gun carriages], tanks and aeroplanes; and the chemical works demoted their energies to the production of the deadly TNT. All the people in the city became absorbed by the new national effort.*

R. H. Brazier and E. Sandford, *Birmingham and the Great War*, 1921

2 List seven products mentioned in source 13. For each one show how it can be directly linked to information about changes in fighting methods described in Chapter 3.

3 Would any of the products mentioned be of value in the post-war world?

New technology for the post-war world

Most goods made in wartime disappeared in the mud and smoke of the battlefields. They did not make Britain any better off. However, the country did gain from the cases where wartime industry helped the spread of new technologies.

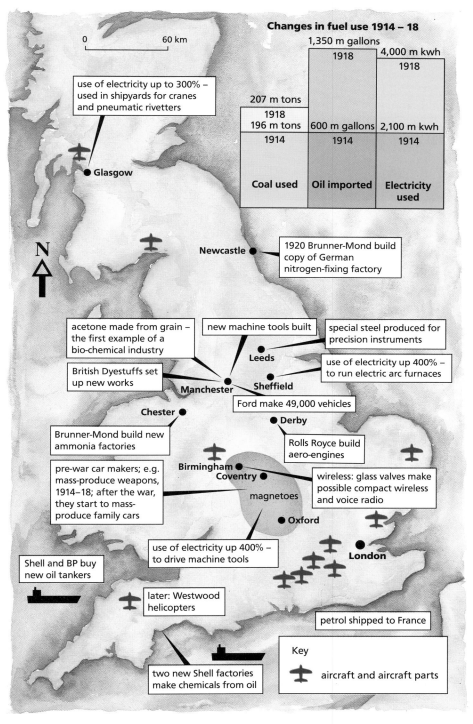

Changes in fuel use 1914 – 18

Coal used	Oil imported	Electricity used
207 m tons 1918	1,350 m gallons 1918	4,000 m kwh 1918
196 m tons 1914	600 m gallons 1914	2,100 m kwh 1914

use of electricity up to 300% – used in shipyards for cranes and pneumatic rivetters

N

● Glasgow

● Newcastle — 1920 Brunner-Mond build copy of German nitrogen-fixing factory

acetone made from grain – the first example of a bio-chemical industry

new machine tools built

special steel produced for precision instruments

● Leeds

British Dyestuffs set up new works

● Sheffield

use of electricity up 400% – to run electric arc furnaces

● Manchester

Ford make 49,000 vehicles

Chester ●

● Derby

Brunner-Mond build new ammonia factories

Rolls Royce build aero-engines

pre-war car makers; e.g. mass-produce weapons, 1914–18; after the war, they start to mass-produce family cars

Birmingham ●
Coventry ●

magnetoes

wireless: glass valves make possible compact wireless and voice radio

● Oxford

use of electricity up 400% – to drive machine tools

● London

Shell and BP buy new oil tankers

later: Westwood helicopters

petrol shipped to France

two new Shell factories make chemicals from oil

Key

✈ aircraft and aircraft parts

14 New technology in wartime Britain.

4 **How did the Great War encourage the growth of new industry in the Midlands and the South?**

5 **Which wartime needs encouraged the changes in the chemical industry?**

6 **Why were aircraft factories mostly in the South?**

7 **Use the map and your knowledge of fighting on the Western Front to explain the changes shown in the diagram on fuel use.**

Up to 1914, firms which used electric power usually made it in their own small generators. Wartime factories, however, were more likely to buy it from a power station with more powerful generators. This was an important step towards linking all the country's electricity in a 'national grid', which began in 1926.

15 Thermionic valves were used in this army radio, 1918.

16 The De Havilland light bomber was one of the most used civil planes in the 1920s.

The war gave a tremendous boost to air travel too. In 1919 there was a huge aircraft industry and 15,000 airmen looking for work. These were the men who started passenger services to France, which then grew into the airlines of the 1920s and 1930s.

Another legacy of the war was mass-produced cars. In 1914 most car manufacturers made each car separately. Only Ford's factory in Manchester used conveyor belts to carry parts of cars to workers who each carried out one job as they moved past. Ford made the largest number of wartime vehicles. After the war, Austin in Birmingham and Morris in Oxford joined Ford in mass-producing family cars.

Advances in medicine

The war caused appalling wounds and injuries. The sheer number of casualties caused by shelling and gas attacks also stretched the medical services to their

17 Wounded men like these at Dover were a common sight on docks and railway platforms. The endless stream of terrible injuries during the war led to many improvements in medicine.

limits. There were only a few new methods of treatment, as a result of the war, but there was a great speed-up in the use of pre-war discoveries.

Blood transfusions, for example, had already been given for about a hundred years. Most patients died shortly afterwards. Just before the war the reason for this was discovered: blood can be grouped into different types and each patient needs blood from someone of the same blood group. During the war thousands of lives were saved by blood transfusions, especially at Casualty Clearing Stations. At first the only safe method was arm-to-arm transfusions, until an American army doctor found a way of storing blood.

Rifleman Charlie Shepherd described an early arm-to-arm blood transfusion:

18 *I've still got the scar where they opened me up to get the tube into the vein . . . there it was running into the other chap's left arm. He lost a leg – been down in No Man's Land. Gangrene had set in and they'd had to amputate. Oh, he was like death. As white as a sheet . . . I was lying watching the other bloke and, believe me, you could see the colour coming into that man's face.*

C. Shepherd, quoted in L. Macdonald, *Roses of No Man's Land*, 1980

X-Rays had been discovered in 1895, but X-ray machines were still rare in 1913. Hundreds of extra ones were made in the war to help doctors find pieces of shell in mangled bodies. They became standard equipment in post-war hospitals.

Before the war most people were vaccinated only against smallpox. But many soldiers in the trenches were dying from typhus or tetanus. Tetanus caused 32 out of every 1,000 deaths on the Western Front in the first year of war. So from 1915, troops were vaccinated against both typhus and tetanus. The death rate from tetanus dropped to 2 in every 1,000 deaths. Vaccination became much more routine in the post-war years.

Many soldiers returned from war, mutilated by shelling. Many had to have limbs amputated. Often this was the best way to prevent the spread of gangrene. Amputations and artificial limbs were not new. Ex-sailors could sometimes be seen with wooden legs, or hooks instead of hands. However, the war years saw great advances in dealing with such injuries, and the advent of artificial limbs with moving joints.

Plastic surgery, on the other hand, was a completely new area of medicine. Men who came back from the Front with horrific face wounds were patched up at a specialist hospital in London. Before the development of cosmetic surgery, little could be done for badly-mutilated soldiers, except to provide them with masks. But surgeons soon learned to rebuild noses, for example, with bits of bone taken from a rib. They also discovered how to graft skin from one part of the body to another.

Review and Assessment

1 Look at sources 5–12 on women and the war effort. List: (i) four different ways in which women gained from wartime work; (ii) four different kinds of hardship women met.

For each of the answers, give an example from one or more of the sources.

2 **a** Explain which of the gains you think was most important for women (i) at the time and (ii) in the long term.

 b Which group or groups of women gained most from the war? Which gained least? How would you explain the difference?

3 These are some things which happened in the period after the war, from 1919 to 1939:

- Margaret Bondfield became a Cabinet Minister in Britain in 1929.
- Amy Johnson was the first person to fly solo from England to Australia in 1930.
- The first Penguin paperback book was published in 1935.
- In 1921 there was a ratio of 638 females : 362 males over the age of 14. This compared with a ratio of 595 females : 405 males in 1911.
- The number of cars rose from 1 per 232 people in 1919 to 1 per 15 people in 1939.
- Employment in mining fell on average 2 per cent a year; in electrical production it rose nearly 4 per cent a year.
- The proportion of girls going to grammar school rose from 11 per cent to 17 per cent.
- The population of the Midlands rose nearly four times as much as the population of Lancashire.

For each one, explain whether it is most likely that (i) it could not have happened but for the Great War; (ii) the Great War might have made the change come earlier; (iii) the Great War made no difference.

4 Look back at Chapters 3 and 4. Copy this table, allowing space to make notes. Complete the table with information from Chapters 3 and 4.

	Metal industry	Chemical industry	Transport	Communications	Medicine
a) Changes directly caused by the war					
b) Changes speeded up by the war					
c) Developments of post-war value					
d) Developments without post-war value					

5 Discussion:

- Which wartime inventions or developments have had the greatest effect on our lives today?
- For many people, such as women working in munitions factories, their new wartime jobs lasted only until 1918. What effects might the experience of wartime work have had on them?

An island at war

War from the air

Zeppelins and bombers

MEN OF BRITAIN !
WILL YOU STAND THIS ?

PHOTO BY F. FOXTON, SCARBOROUGH

N.º 2 Wykeham Street, SCARBOROUGH, after the German bombardment on Dec.ʳ 16ᵗʰ. It was the Home of a Working Man. Four People were killed in this House including the Wife, aged 58, and Two Children, the youngest aged 5.

78 Women & Children were killed and 228 Women & Children were wounded by the German Raiders
ENLIST NOW

1   **Why do you think this photograph was used on a recruiting poster?**

2   **What effect would a recruiting poster like this have on the British people?**

3   **When was the last time that a foreign enemy had killed people in England?**

1   A photograph of the bomb damage at Scarborough used on a recruiting poster.

The east coast of England came into the front line in December 1914. German battle-cruisers shelled Scarborough and Hartlepool. On 19 January 1915 the first Zeppelin airship appeared over Yarmouth. Its bombs killed four people.

2 The Zeppelin, a cylinder-shaped airship, was named after the Count von Zeppelin who first designed and produced it.

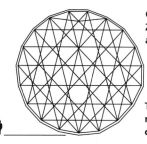

Cross-section of a Zeppelin, showing its aluminium frame

The frame held gas cells made of cow's skin and cotton

Zeppelin LZ62 (L30)
volume/gas content: 55,194 cubic metres
length: 198 m
diameter: 24 m
engines: six 240 hp
load: 32,500kg
max. speed: 100 kmph
max. height: 5,400 m
cruising range: 3,700 km

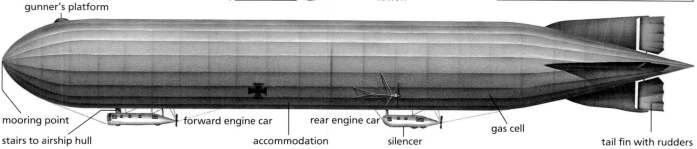

gunner's platform

mooring point

stairs to airship hull

forward engine car

accommodation

rear engine car

silencer

gas cell

tail fin with rudders

4 Roughly, how does this airship compare with the size of your classroom?

5 Refer to sources 2 and 3. Why were Zeppelins, and not aeroplanes, used as bombers in 1914 and 1915? (Chapter 3, pages 35–41 may also help you.)

6 What did Slessor mean by 'a cod's eye view of the Queen Mary' (source 3)? What does it suggest about what the Zeppelin was like?

7 Many people of the time thought that the main form of air travel of the future would be by airship. What evidence is there in sources 3 and 4 that airships were more advanced than aeroplanes?

Before the war, airships had carried 35,000 passengers between German cities without accident. Now the Zeppelin had become a bomber. In the next two years, they came 50 times, killing more than 500 people and injuring over 1,300.

At first there was little the Royal Flying Corps, or RFC, could do. A young pilot, John Slessor (who later became Chief of the RAF) flew up in a plane to meet a Zeppelin in September 1915:

3 *I was climbing to my 10,000 feet* [3,000 metres] *which one thought was a fabulous height in those days and . . . there, lit up by the glare of the lights from London, was this enormous thing. I suppose, 1,000 or 2,000 feet* [3–600 metres] *above me. It looked like a cod's eye view of the Queen Mary* [an ocean liner] *. . . When I was climbing towards him* [the Zeppelin], *I suddenly saw a trail of sparks come out of each of his four engines and he then started to move forward and cocked himself up to an almost unbelievable angle . . . and he just left me standing.*

John Slessor, interview with Peter Liddle, *The Airman's War*, 1987

4 'The Underworld': the Elephant
and Castle tube station in London
during a Zeppelin air raid.
Painting by Walter Bayes, 1918.

1 Who does the artist Walter
Bayes suggest were most likely
to seek shelter (source 4)?
2 What does the painting show
about the effect of air raids?
3 Do you think he is sympathetic
to the people he has painted?
4 The deaths from air raids were
tiny compared with deaths at
the Front – or from the Blitz
(heavy bombing in the Second
World War). Why should so
many people have been terrified
of the air raids?

As a measure against Zeppelin raids, councils turned off street-lighting in towns and cities, and ordered householders to black-out lighted windows. Anti-aircraft guns and searchlights were set up around towns. Wireless stations listened in to the Zeppelin's signals. By the end of 1916 a dozen Zeppelins had been shot down.

The Germans stopped sending airships, but they now had night-bombers – aeroplanes like the twin-engined Gotha and the four-engined Giant (see also page 41). Most raids were aimed at London. The capital was ringed with airfields for night-fighters. In May 1918, British bombers shot down seven Gothas, and the German air attacks stopped – but they had by then already killed 1,162 and injured 4,000.

War at sea

The British blockade of ports

Food and raw materials for industry were as vital to winning the war as soldiers, sailors and airmen. Before the war, both Britain and Germany had relied on imports of raw materials and food. These supplies arrived from all over the world by ship. From August 1914, Britain decided to use ships of the Royal Navy to blockade the entrances to German ports. This would prevent supplies from overseas countries reaching Germany's industries and people.

5 The naval blockade of Germany.

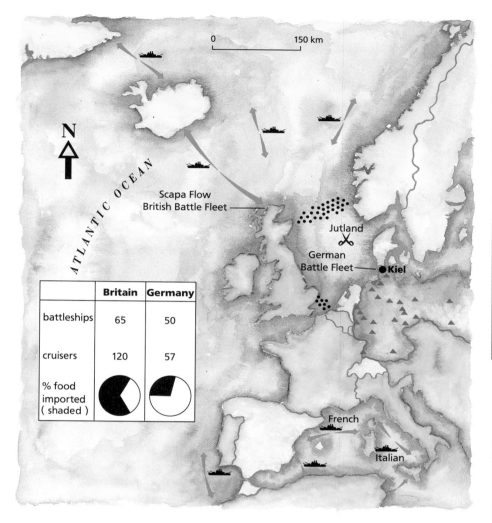

	Britain	Germany
battleships	65	50
cruisers	120	57
% food imported (shaded)		

Key

Warship patrols stop all ships. Those going to neutral countries allowed through if their cargoes are not for Germany.

Battle of Jutland, June 1916. Both navies lose ships but the Germans fail to destroy the British fleet. The German fleet stays in Kiel harbour for the rest of the war.

minefields

towns where there were food riots, 1916

Allied Powers

Central Powers

neutral countries

5 Look at source 6. What nationality is the ship being stopped? Why is it going to be searched?

6 Use the information in the map (source 5) and picture (source 6) to explain how a 'blockade' worked.

7 Why was Scapa Flow a good base for the British battle fleet?

6 'Lower Away', a painting by James Shaw, on board HMS *Changuinola*. The ship in the distance is going to be inspected for 'contraband' – goods that were not allowed to be supplied to the enemy.

The blockade soon started to have an effect. Germans remembered 1916–17 as the 'turnip winter' because that was the only food most could get to eat. An American reporter observed queues waiting for hours to get their weekly ration of a single egg:

7 *There was not one who had had enough to eat for weeks. In the case of the younger women and children the skin was drawn hard to the bones and bloodless. Eyes had fallen deeper into the sockets. From the lips all color was gone . . .*

George E. Schreiner, *The Iron Ration*, 1918

1 **What do the map (source 5) and George Schreiner (source 7) tell you about the success of the blockade?**

2 **How would food shortages affect Germany's war effort?**

The U-boat campaign

Germany could win only if it forced Britain to suffer the same shortages. It needed to cut Britain off from its empire and the USA, the main supplier of raw materials and equipment. Yet the German Navy's surface ships could not leave port to blockade Britain. It had to rely on the *Untersee boot*, or 'U'-boat, a submarine which slipped unseen under the surface into the Atlantic. U-boats could not capture ships, only sink them with torpedoes or guns. In 1915, German submarine sinkings of cargo ships on their way to Britain became a major threat to the British war effort. If no Royal Navy ship was nearby, the German U-boat would give the crew time to take to the lifeboats. If speed was necessary, they sank the ship without warning. A Punch cartoon summed up a British view of U-boats and their crews:

In May 1915, a U-boat sank the British liner, *Lusitania*, which was carrying war supplies as well as passengers. There were 110 Americans among the 1,100 people drowned. The USA, which was neutral at this time, protested strongly. The last thing Germany wanted was to bring them into the war. So U-boats were ordered to stop sinkings on sea-lanes used by Americans.

On other sea-lanes, German U-boats went on sinking ships. The USA was Britain's biggest supplier, though. By the winter of 1916–17 the British were not starving, and the Germans were. Germany was desperate. On 1 February 1917 it opened 'unrestricted' submarine warfare. American ships became targets again.

8 Cartoon from *Punch*, 1915.

PUNCH, OR THE LONDON CHARIVARI.—April 7, 1915.

A GREAT NAVAL TRIUMPH.

GERMAN SUBMARINE OFFICER. "THIS OUGHT TO MAKE **THEM** JEALOUS IN THE SISTER SERVICE. BELGIUM SAW NOTHING BETTER THAN **THIS.**"

Look carefully at source 8.

3 Describe in detail the story the picture is telling.

4 The ship appears to be a merchant ship. Which detail does that make unlikely?

5 In the caption, the officer's 'sister service' is the Army. Explain the point of what he is saying about Belgium.

6 How would a German submarine officer defend his action in letting people drown?

7 Propaganda has to be believable if it is to work. Explain how this could be believable to British readers in 1915.

The Germans knew that the USA would now declare war, but they had calculated that their 100 U-boats could sink 600,000 tonnes of shipping a month. This would have a dreadful effect on the Allies. Britain would have to surrender before the Americans could send an army to France.

The United States did as the Germans expected. On 7 April 1917, President Wilson declared war. Meanwhile, the British did something unexpected. They gathered their ships sailing to and from Britain and formed *convoys*. A convoy consisted of slow-moving merchant ships, escorted by anti-submarine destroyers and armed merchant ships or trawlers. Convoys made it increasingly difficult for U-boats to find targets, and to attack them.

1 How long did it take for the
U-boats to reach their target of
monthly sinkings?
2 Explain what the table shows
about the value of the convoy
system.
3 The convoys' main success was
not in sinking U-boats but in
making it more difficult for
them to find merchant ships.
Explain why this was.

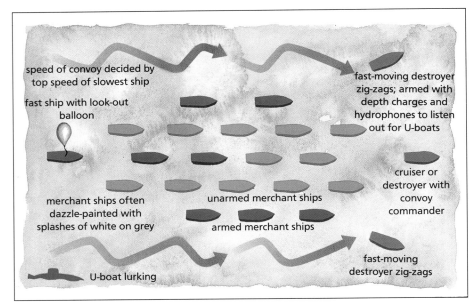

9 The convoy system, introduced in
May 1917.

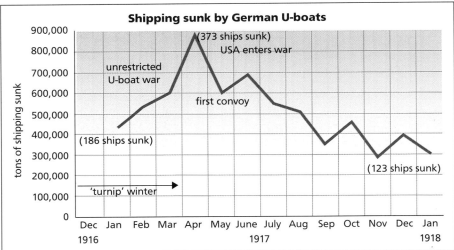

How well was Britain fed?

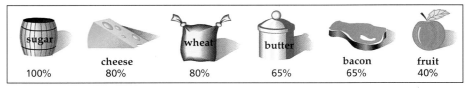

10 Proportions of food imported in 1913.

4 What problems would this lead
to in wartime?
5 Which of these imports might
be replaced by home-produced
food?

Convoys stopped about half of the sinkings, but German U-boats still
succeeded in reducing Britain's food supplies. This forced the Government to
increase the amount of home-grown food. Again women were called on. In
1917 the Government formed the Women's Land Army. Thousands of women

were recruited to work in one of the three sections: agriculture; timber cutting; and forage (looking after foodstuffs for animals). The Government also urged townspeople and householders to turn their parks and gardens into allotments for vegetables.

From 1917 there was also a 'plough-up' campaign. Scientists advised that bread and potatoes could give calories in place of other foods such as meat. Farmers were therefore given good prices for corn if they grew it on land which had been used for grazing animals. 'Government loaves' were made with two-thirds wheat-flour and one-third flour made from maize, barley and potatoes. It was not tasty but the price was cut from 12 to 9*d* (old pence) for a 4lb loaf.

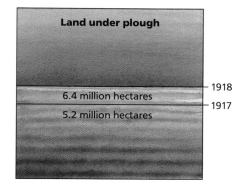

11 Land under plough.

12 Recruiting poster for the Women's Land Army, 1917.

6 Why do you think the name 'Land Army' was chosen?

7 Which other forms of National Service for women were started in spring 1917?

8 How does the picture (source 12) show an important part of the Government's food policy?

9 What does it tell you about agricultural technology?

10 Look at source 14. How would people help the war effort by eating less bread?

There were still shortages of other foods. Between January and June 1917 47,000 tonnes of meat and 87,000 tonnes of sugar went to the sea bed. Food merchants put up prices and people spent long hours in 'queues' – a new word in the language.

13 *Outside the dairy shops of certain multiple firms in some parts of London women began to line up for margarine as early as 5 o'clock on Saturday morning, some with infants in their arms . . . in Walworth Road in the south-eastern side of London the queue was stated to number about 3,000. Two hours later 1,000 of these were sent away unsupplied.*

The Times, 10 December 1917

14 Government poster, 1917. Posters like this urged people to cater carefully.

15 Chart showing rationing in 1918. From the *Illustrated London News*.

Examine source 15.

1 Which would be the most serious food deficiencies in Germany?

2 How would you use this chart to illustrate a talk on the sea blockades in the Great War?

3 How do the pictures support what the text says about rationing in Germany, Austria and Britain?

4 The magazine obviously intended this to give boost to its readers' spirits. Does this make it propaganda? Explain your view.

5 Give as many kinds of reason as you can why Britain won the Blockade War.

Some towns set up rationing schemes and found that the queues disappeared once everyone was sure that they would get a share. In February 1918 the Government first introduced rationing for scarce foods such as butter and margarine. *The Illustrated London News* (left) compared rations in Britain with those of its enemies.

Living in wartime Britain

A healthier nation?

Before the war many surveys showed that about one in five people lived below the 'poverty line'. They could not afford enough food, warmth and damp-free housing for their children to grow up healthily. The results were seen at the outbreak of war, when doctors examined 2.5 million men to see if they were fit for the Armed Forces:

> **16** *Of every nine men of military age in Great Britain, on the average three were perfect, fit, and healthy; two were on a definitely inferior plane of health and strength; three . . . could almost (in view of their age) be described . . . as physical wrecks; and the remaining man was a chronic invalid.*
>
> C. Smith, *Britain's Food Supplies in Peace and War*, 1921

6 Explain the connection between these findings in source 16 and the numbers of people below the poverty line before the war?

The greatest poverty and ill-health were found among people without full-time work. The war soon ended unemployment, though. For example, a charity in Leicester gave free meals and clothing to the jobless every winter, but in December 1914 no one came for help as the town's factories had been given orders for 4 million pairs of army boots. With full-time jobs, some of the poorest people could now afford decent food, clothes and heating.

There was even more chance of rising above the poverty line when the drive for munitions started in 1915. Women gave up working as household servants for £10 a year, and went into factories to be paid £2 or £3 a week instead. Boys and girls under 18 were paid near-adult wages. Wartime reports described the effects these changes had on the general health of children:

1 Why did the population increase in munitions areas (source 17)?

2 How many extra people did the stores employ (source 17)? How would this be evidence for a higher standard of living?

3 Explain the link between sources 17 and 18.

> **17** *In munitions areas, owing to the high rate of wages, combined with increased population, the demand for goods has increased. This is well illustrated by the large growth in the number of persons employed in co-operative and departmental stores. Although there are 30,000 fewer males employed than before the war, the females have increased by nearly 86,000.*

Board of Trade Report on the State of Employment, July 1918

> **18** *The evidence from school doctors and the Board's medical inspectors in all parts of the country is to the effect that in 1916 the children were, on the whole, better fed and clothed than at any time since medical inspection was introduced* [in 1907].

Government's Chief Medical Officer, Annual Report for 1916

It was more difficult to improve medical care because so many doctors and nurses were in the Armed Forces. But people began to be more concerned for the health of infants and their mothers, especially now that so many women were helping in the war effort. A bishop put it this way in July 1917:

> While nine soldiers died every hour in 1915, twelve babies died every hour so that it was more dangerous to be a baby than a soldier. The loss of life in this war has made every baby's life doubly precious.

During the war, the number of health visitors went up from 600 to 1,355, and compulsory training was started for midwives. A few local councils opened the first mother and child clinics. These were the small beginnings of the mother and child services which spread widely in the years after the war.

NATIONAL BABY WEEK
July 1st–7th, 1917.

President
THE RT. HON. DAVID LLOYD GEORGE.
Chairman of the Council
THE RT. HON. LORD RHONDDA.
Vice-Chairman of the Council : THE HON. Waldorf Astor, M.P.
Chairman of the Executive Committee : Dr Eric Pritchard.
Vice-Chairman of the Executive Committee : Mrs A. C. Gotto.
Hon. Secretary : Miss Wrench.
Hon. Treasurer : W. Hardy, Esq.
Secretary : Miss Alice Elliott.

SAVE THE BABIES
RE-BUILD THE NATION AND EMPIRE

"The Race marches forward on the feet of Little Children."

NATIONAL BABY WEEK, KINGSWAY HOUSE, KINGSWAY. W.C. 2.
TELEPHONE : REGENT 1890

19 Poster advertising the National Baby Week in July 1917. It drew people's attention to the importance of protecting babies.

'Homes for heroes'

Before the war, Medical Officers had shown that overcrowded slums were the main cause of diseases such as tuberculosis (TB), and childhood illnesses like diptheria and measles which could then be deadly. During the war, hardly any houses were built. Builders were either in the Army or constructing new munitions factories.

In 1917 Lloyd George became Prime Minister instead of Herbert Asquith. His first aim was to win the war, but he also looked ahead to the day when he would have to fight a General Election. He set up a Ministry of Reconstruction to plan for a new post-war Britain. It drew up schemes for

4 Explain the connection between overcrowded homes and poor health.

government money to help local councils build houses. As Lloyd George put it in the 1919 General Election: the aim was to build 'Homes for Heroes'. The years 1920 and 1921 saw the start of large-scale council-house building.

The hardships of wartime

In 1914 shops put up signs saying 'business as usual'. Theatres and cinemas stayed open. Football and racing continued. But in 1915, life became tougher. League football, county cricket and racing ended with the Cup Final. As Lord Derby handed over the Cup he said, 'You have played with one another and against one another for the Cup; play with one another for England now.'

Before the war, pubs had been open from 5 or 6 a.m. until around midnight. The Government feared that soldiers and workmen would turn up the next day with hangovers. So it cut opening hours to two-and-a-half hours in the middle of the day and to three in the evening. It put heavier taxes on drink and brought down the strength of beer. People were forbidden to buy each other drinks (called 'treating'). The numbers of people convicted of drunkenness each week – both men and women – fell from 3,888 in 1914 to 449 in 1918. A Medical Officer also reported that:

21 *The practice of gangs of men congregating in public houses, which used to be a common feature the whole day through, is much less frequent, and this is attributed to the 'Treating Clauses' in the Order.*

Medical Officer of Health, Liverpool, 1915

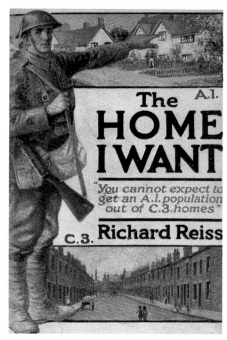

20 The cover of a book published in 1918.

5 'A1' and 'C3' were the highest and lowest grades that doctors gave to men when they examined them for fitness to serve in the Army. How does the book cover (source 20) use A1 and C3?

6 Can you think of a reason why wartime drunkenness might have risen if it had not been for the new laws?

7 If most people convicted of drunkenness were younger men, why might the numbers have fallen during the war?

The dark years of the war came in 1916. The Government cancelled Whitsun and August Bank Holidays so that munitions productions would go on uninterrupted. Guy Fawkes Night was banned. Petrol became scarce; many vans were fitted with bags holding methane and powered by gas instead. Timber was in short supply so newspapers became thinner, and matches disappeared from shops.

The Government began to demand more money from people. In 1914 only about one million people paid income tax. By 1918 the number had risen

22 New Year message to 'All at Home', *Punch* 1918.

1 List the difficulties those at home would have to 'stick'.

2 How does source 23 explain how the Press Bureau worked.

3 Was the Government concerned only about giving information to Germany?

4 Discuss the arguments a) for and b) against censoring news and pictures about air raids?

5 How could this affect the way the correspondents reported the war?

to six million. If people had any savings left, the Government wanted them to buy War Bonds or War Savings Certificates – this was the start of National Savings Certificates.

Travel became more difficult as the Army took engines to France and filled the trains in Britain with its soldiers. At the same time, motor buses began to wear out. Britain had more men and women at work than ever before. Often the transport system could not cope. The hardships deepened further in the winter of 1917–18 as this Punch cartoon shows.

Censorship and propaganda

By the time of the Great War, nearly everyone could read. Reporters were always on the look-out for stories for the popular newspapers. However, politicians and army leaders feared that information in the newspapers might pass to the enemy. The truth about the war might also lead to panic at home. At the beginning of the war, therefore, DORA gave the Government power to to control information. DORA, as everyone called 'her', was the Defence of the Realm Act. The Act allowed the Government to take all sorts of high-handed actions in the 'national interest'. These included things such as closing pubs, taking over railways, rationing food and setting up the Press Bureau to censor news and to guide newspapers on what to print. Here is an example of one of many Press Bureau orders:

23 *It is undesirable that too much space* [in newspapers] *should be given to describing Zeppelin raids.*

. . . So long as the Germans think that the raids have great effect they will be continued, and long accounts tend to produce an impression both in England and Germany that they are of greater importance than they are in reality . . .

Press Bureau Order, 1915

At first newspaper correspondents were not allowed to join the Army in France. From 1915 they could go to the Front, but they were taken around by censors from the Press Bureau. After the war, one censor described how:

24 *When the autumn twilight came down on the haggard trenchwork world . . . they* [the war correspondents] *would be speeding west in Vauxhall cars to lighted chateaux gleaming white among scatheless* [undamaged] *woods.*

C. E. Montagu, *Disenchantment*, 1922

6 For each picture (sources 25–28), make a list of ways in which it provides: **a)** good evidence (direct or indirect) about the fighting; **b)** misleading information.

7 Why do you think Bruce Bairnsfather's cartoons were popular with troops?

8 Discuss the arguments for and against censoring pictures.

Official war artists included young painters like Paul Nash (source 17, page 38) who had been soldiers. Some of their paintings were shown in exhibitions but few people saw them. The Army had photographers at the Front, but the only pictures which appeared in newspapers were 'official' ones such as scenes of the King or Prime Minister visiting troops behind the Front. None of the photographs of battle scenes in this book were seen during the war.

Censorship was one way to influence people. The other was propaganda. The main form of propaganda was government posters but there was also a new one. In 1917 a government report wrote that, 'half of the entire population, men, women and children, visit a cinematograph theatre once a week.' Just as today, most of the films at the cinema came from America. But there were also 'official' films made by the Government, like *The Battle of the Somme* (see source 4, page 76.

One result of censorship and propaganda was that few people had any idea of what it was like to fight in France.

Images of the war.

25 A government poster, seen by millions.

26 'Well if you knows of a better 'ole, go to it.' Cartoon drawn by the soldiers' favourite cartoonist, Captain Bruce Bairnsfather.

27 'Paths of Glory', a painting by the war artist C. R. Nevinson. This was censored in 1918 because it showed death, which was against a DORA regulation.

28 Stretcher-bearers carrying a wounded man through the mud at the Battle of Passchendaele (see page 79). This photograph was not seen during the war.

Look at source 29.

1 What was the tribunal member trying to discover?

2 Suggest reasons why his question was: a) fair; b) unfair.

3 Is there anything which suggests the member was biased against conscientious objectors?

Refusing to fight

In 1914 most politicians believed that not having conscription was a sign that Britain had a more free society than other European countries. In 1916 they changed their minds because of the need for a still bigger army. Conscription began – but there was one important difference from the continent.

The conscription law allowed people to be 'conscientious objectors' if their conscience said it was wrong to kill under any circumstance. To be accepted as a conscientious objector, a man had to apply to a tribunal of councillors and local leaders. Their questions were not meant to be easy:

29
MEMBER: *What would you do if a German attacked your mother?*

APPLICANT: *If possible I would get between the attacker and my mother but under no circumstances would I take a life to save life.*

MEMBER: *If the only way to save your mother were to kill a German, would you still let him kill her?*

APPLICANT: *Yes.*

MEMBER: *You ought to be shot.*

Bradford Daily Telegraph, 16 March 1916

If the tribunal decided the man was a conscientious objector, they offered him the chance to serve his country by labouring work or in an ambulance team. About 10,000 agreed to do this. Another 6,000 were 'absolutists'. They absolutely refused to help the business of fighting in any way.

It needed great courage to be an absolutist. They were arrested and taken to an army camp. If they refused to put on uniform, they were given a court martial and sentenced to an army prison. Howard Marten, an absolutist, smuggled out an account of how they were treated:

30
We were placed in handcuffs and locked in the cells and tied up for two hours in the afternoon. We were tied up by the wrists to horizontal ropes about five feet [1.5 metres] off the ground with our arms outstretched and our feet tied together. Then we were confined to our cells for three days on 'punishment diet' (four biscuits a day and water) . . .

Quoted in S. Davies, *The Home Front*, 1976

4 What does source 30 tell you about the strength of absolutists' beliefs?

5 How does it help to explain how 71 conscientious objectors died as a result of their treatment?

6 Discuss the 'pros' and 'cons' of conscientious objection in: a) any war; b) the Great War.

Review and Assessment

1 Look at the cartoon (source 22) on page 70. Copy and complete the table below, using information from Chapters 4 and 5. Assess whether people of 1918 would be able to 'stick it' in these areas:

Area	For sticking it	Against sticking it	Something on both sides
Food Work and wages Health Housing Air raids Leisure Travel			

2 What were the main effects of the Great War on life in Britain 1914–1918? Use your notes from the table to write your own account.

3 Describe the main ways in which the Government tried to keep people in Britain on its side during the war. How far do you think it succeeded with (i) munitions workers; (ii) housewives; (iii) conscientious objectors; (iv) magazines such as *Punch* and *Illustrated London News*?

4 Read these three statements on the use of gas in warfare:

> In 1907, an international conference at the Hague banned 'the use of projectiles, the sole purpose of which is the spread of asphyxicating or harmful gas.' (Hague Convention, Article 27)

> On 22 April 1915, the British Cabinet agreed 'that he [Lord Kitchener] should use anything he could get invented.'

> On 29 April 1915, *The Times*: 'An atrocious method of warfare . . . this diabolical invention [gas] . . . will fill all races with a horror of the German name.'

a Suggest reasons why the Hague Convention tried to ban gas, but not other weapons such as high explosives.

b From information in Chapter 3, page 39, say what happened a few hours before the British Cabinet's decision. What effect would this have had on the Cabinet's decision?

c Give reasons which could be used for and against the decision.

d Is it probable that *The Times* knew of the Cabinet decision? If they had, would their comment be justified in any way?

6 Europe and the world at war

War on the Western Front 1915–17

From December 1914, both sides dug themselves into trenches, and so began a long war of 'attrition', or 'wearing down'. Through 1915, the armies facing each other in Belgium and France tried to build up their strength for the great 'push' which they believed would break the defences and the spirit of the enemy. The British line was held by the remaining men of the BEF who were joined by Territorials, or part-time soldiers, and some regiments from India and Canada. Back in Britain, the millions of volunteers for Kitchener's New Army were being trained, and the drive to produce more guns and shells began in the spring.

The year 1915 saw the beginnings of a frightfulness which marked the rest of the war. In just four battles the British lost 159,000 men, killed or wounded. That was one-and-a-half times the number of men who had gone to France in the BEF in August 1914. All their sacrifice had gained was a few villages. This lack of success led the British Government to sack the Commander-in-Chief, Sir John French, and put Douglas Haig in charge.

By the summer of 1916 General Haig had taken over 120 kilometres of trench and he now commanded 1.5 million men; more would arrive soon, now that conscription had started in Britain. He was ready to join in the fighting on the same scale as the French and Germans who were already locked in the Battle of Verdun.

Verdun was a pre-war French fortress – several square kilometres of steel and reinforced concrete buildings. It stood in a salient – a part of the front line which jutted out towards Germany. The Germans believed the French would defend Verdun to the last man. 'If they do so', wrote their

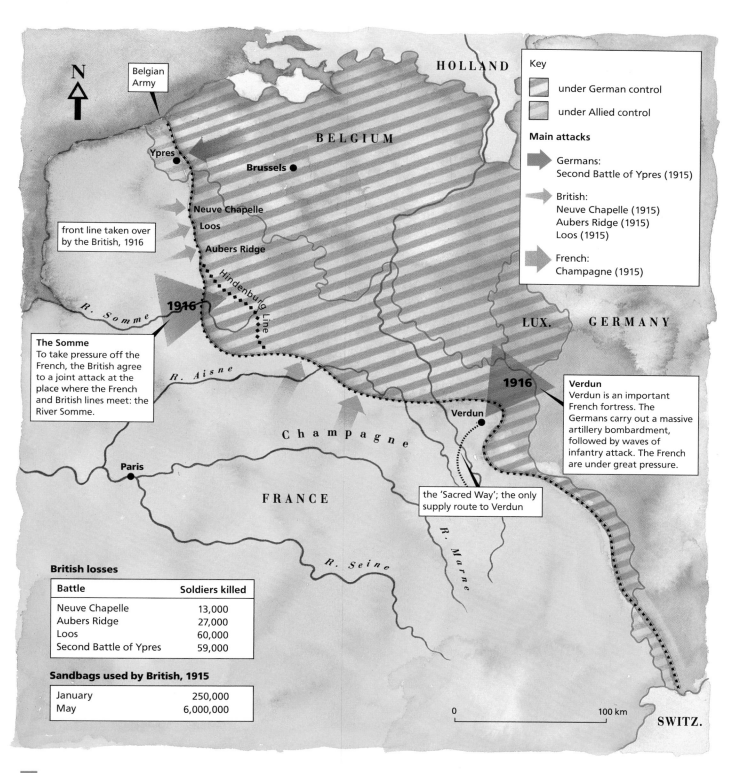

The Western Front, 1915–16.

Key

| | under German control |
| | under Allied control |

Main attacks

Germans:
Second Battle of Ypres (1915)

British:
Neuve Chapelle (1915)
Aubers Ridge (1915)
Loos (1915)

French:
Champagne (1915)

front line taken over by the British, 1916

Belgian Army

The Somme
To take pressure off the French, the British agree to a joint attack at the place where the French and British lines meet: the River Somme.

Verdun
Verdun is an important French fortress. The Germans carry out a massive artillery bombardment, followed by waves of infantry attack. The French are under great pressure.

the 'Sacred Way'; the only supply route to Verdun

British losses

Battle	Soldiers killed
Neuve Chapelle	13,000
Aubers Ridge	27,000
Loos	60,000
Second Battle of Ypres	59,000

Sandbags used by British, 1915

January	250,000
May	6,000,000

Commander-in-Chief, 'the Forces of France will bleed to death.' The French General Petain's reply was, 'They will not pass.' The French made great sacrifices, but Verdun might have fallen if Haig had not forced the Germans to move men away from Verdun, by starting a battle at the River Somme.

1 Which weapon would have killed most of the soldiers?

2 How did the method of attack make it easy for the Germans?

The tragedy of the Somme, June–November 1916

In the last week of June a British General spoke to a rifle battalion. A soldier describes what was said:

> 2   *He told us of the coming great advance . . . that might mean the end of the war . . . These guns, both large and small, would shell the German positions until they were flat, and not a single German soldier would be left in them.*
>
> George Ashurst, *My Bit*, 1987

In that week, 50,000 British gunners fired three million high explosives and gas shells from guns placed every seventeen metres along a distance of twenty-four kilometres. But things did not happen as the General had promised. Most of the German enemy were in dug-outs, ten metres underground. They were still alive on 1 July when the guns stopped at 7.30 a.m. and 60,000 British troops clambered out from their trenches. Each soldier had a rifle, 220 rounds of ammunition, two gas helmets, two grenades, a first-aid pack and iron rations. Most also carried a wire-cutter, a spade, a signal flare, even a roll of barbed wire. A Brigadier's diary described their fate:

> 3   *I see rows upon rows of British soldiers lying dead, dying or wounded in No Man's Land. Here and there I see an officer urging on his followers. Occasionally I can see the hands thrown up and then a body flops to the ground . . . Thiepval village is still held . . . it is now 8 a.m. and by 7.45 a.m. it should have fallen.*
>
> Brigadier Crozier, 1916, quoted in J. Terraine, *The Great War*, 1965

In that 30 minutes, half of the 60,000 British troops were killed or wounded. By nightfall 120,000 had gone 'over the top' into the hail of shells and machine-gun-fire. Now 20,000 were dead and 37,000 wounded.

3 The scene in source 4 was shot behind the Front. Find three clues which show it was not the actual battle scene.

4 Even if it were faked, how well does this portray the first day of the battle?

4   Scene from the government film, *The Battle of the Somme*. It was shown in August 1916.

The fighting at the Somme went on for 140 days. It can be divided into eight smaller battles. Most were British 'victories' because they captured a wood, a village or a ridge. But the victories did not lead to a breakthrough. In places, the Allies had won about ten kilometres; in others, less than three. Everywhere they had finally shattered the enemy trench system, but the Germans simply moved back just a few kilometres to a much stronger line of trenches which were easier to defend. The British called these trenches the 'Hindenburg Line' (see map, page 75).

The Somme: a turning point in the war

In the first days of fighting the newspapers carried reports of British victories. A few days later they were printing long lists of dead. There were so many wounded soldiers that they had to be brought in trains as far north as Rochdale, as a Volunteer Aid Detachment nurse remembered:

> **5** . . . *One* [of the wounded] *would be helping another, and some of the better ones were pushing some of the other chaps in bathchairs . . . The roads were lined with people watching and rushing into their houses and out again to give them drinks of water, barley, squash, biscuits, chocolates, cigarettes – anything they had . . . all day long they went past our house up the road to Birch Hill. It was shocking.*

Kathleen Yarwood, VAD, speaking in the 1970s

The Somme was a turning point in how people saw the war. Before, it had almost been a great adventure. Now it was a dreadful sacrifice of young lives. Many blamed the generals for having no idea how to fight a modern war. The beginnings of the change can be traced in newspapers of the first few days of the battle. Look at these two extracts from the *Daily Chronicle*:

> **6** *Our troops, fighting with very splendid valour have swept across the enemy's front, trenches along a great part of the line of attack and have captured villages and strongholds which the Germans have long held . . . Many hundreds of enemy are prisoners in our hands. His dead lie thick in the track of our regiments.*
>
> *Daily Chronicle*, 3 July 1916

> **7** *No man or woman could dare to speak again of war's 'glory' or of 'the splendour of war', or any of those old lying phrases which hide the dreadful truth.*
>
> *Daily Chronicle*, 16 July 1916

5 How could such a change take place in ideas about the war in just two weeks (sources 6 and 7)?

But the battle was a turning point for the Germans too. Two years before, the 100,000 men of the BEF were a 'contemptible little army'. On the Somme, that

1 How does this painting (source 9) give a different picture of the Somme from the government film (source 4)?
2 In which ways does it show how the Somme was a turning point in the war?

same number went into battle each day for nearly four months. They fought with the same weapons as the Germans – heavy artillery, machine guns, gas, and aircraft – as well as one weapon the Germans did not have: the tank. When the Battle of the Somme ended in November, and Verdun in December, the losses from death and injury amounted to a staggering 1.75 million:

8			
Verdun:	French	362,000	
	Germans	336,000	
The Somme:	British	415,000	
	Germans	about 450,000	
	French	195,000	

9 Heavy guns at the Somme, painting by A. C. Michael.

'Hell' at Passchendaele, 1917

By mid 1917, the British share of the fighting had grown once again. General Haig now led 1.8 million men, and the British line stretched for nearly 170 kilometres. The French Army was in danger of collapse after General Nivelle's offensive in April led to so many casualties that there was a widespread mutiny.

Haig decided to open a third battle at Ypres. It followed one of the few clear successes of the war. British miners bored 13 tunnels under Messines Ridge, which was held by the Germans. Inside they packed a million tonnes of explosive, and on 7 June they blew the ridge open with a bang which rattled windows in London. British troops captured what remained of the ridge.

10 Canadian troops hold the line at Passchendaele, 14 November.

4 How does this picture (source 10) help to explain why Haig called off the battle?

5 What does it tell you about the effects of heavy shelling?

Haig now planned to take other ridges around Ypres to open the way for an attack on Belgian ports. The Third Battle of Ypres began on 31 July 1917. This time the British had more than 3,000 guns which fired 4.5 million shells as infantrymen and machine-gunners fought in the mud and almost continual rain. To the troops the battle became known as 'Passchendaele' – the name of the village on the last ridge. Canadians took the heap of rubble that had been Passchendaele on 6 November. Haig then called off the battle because of bad weather, exhausted troops and 247,000 casualties.

Memories of Passchendale: the British

11 *I died in hell – (they called it Passchendaele);*
My wound was slight.
And I was hobbling back and then a shell
Burst slick upon the duckboards; so I fell
Into the bottomless mud, and lost the light.

Siegfried Sassoon, *Memorial Tablet*

12 *For the first time the British Army lost its spirit of optimism, and there was a sense of deadly depression among many officers and men with whom I came in touch.*

Philip Gibbs, *Realities of War*, 1920

13 *The positions already gained fall short of what I had wished to secure before the winter . . . Our present position about Passchendaele . . . may be difficult and costly to hold if seriously attacked.*

General Haig, letter to the Chief of Staff, 15 November 1917

6 Passchendaele was the last of the long battles of attrition. How do sources 11–15 suggest it affected soldiers on both sides?

7 Thousands of soldiers' bodies were never found. How does Sassoon's poem (source 11) reflect this?

8 Compare sources 13 and 15. Is there evidence that the battle was no more than a waste of life? Did either side come out weaker or stronger?

Memories of Passchendaele: the Germans

14 *After crawling out through the bleeding remnants of my comrades and the smoke and debris, and wandering and fleeing in the midst of the raging artillery fire in search of a refuge, I am now awaiting death at any moment. You do not know what Flanders means. Flanders means endless endurance. Flanders mean blood and scraps of human bodies. Flanders means heroic courage and faithfulness, even until death.*

Letter found on dead German soldier, 1917

15 *The battle had led to a vast consumption of German strength. Losses had been so high that they could not be replaced and the fighting strength of battalions, already reduced was further reduced.*

German Official History, *The World War, 1914–18*, 1929–36

The British Empire at war: the Middle East and Africa

In October 1914, Turkey had joined the war on the side of Germany. Britain's first reply to the Turkish move had been the Dardanelles' Campaign to open up supply lines to Russia (see Chapter 2, pages 26–28).

Britain had other important interests in the Middle East too. The British-owned Suez Canal was vital for the sea link with India, and the Persian Gulf was essential for moving oil from the British-owned wells in Persia (modern Iran). To defend these interests and fight the Turkish Empire, Britain called on the people of its own empire in India, Australia and New Zealand. ANZAC troops defended the Suez Canal in Egypt, while Indian soldiers captured the post of Basra in Turkey.

The Indian and British Army then marched north to capture Baghdad. At Ctesiphon they met a larger Turkish army and had to retreat to Kut. In April 1916 the Turks captured Kut and took 10,000 Allied prisoners. Two-thirds died in captivity.

The Arab revolt

By 1915 Britain saw it could link the war against the Turks with the Arabs' own struggle to free their lands from Turkish rule. One of the most respected Arab leaders was Sharif Hussein of Mecca. In 1915 the British promised Hussein

16 The Middle East.

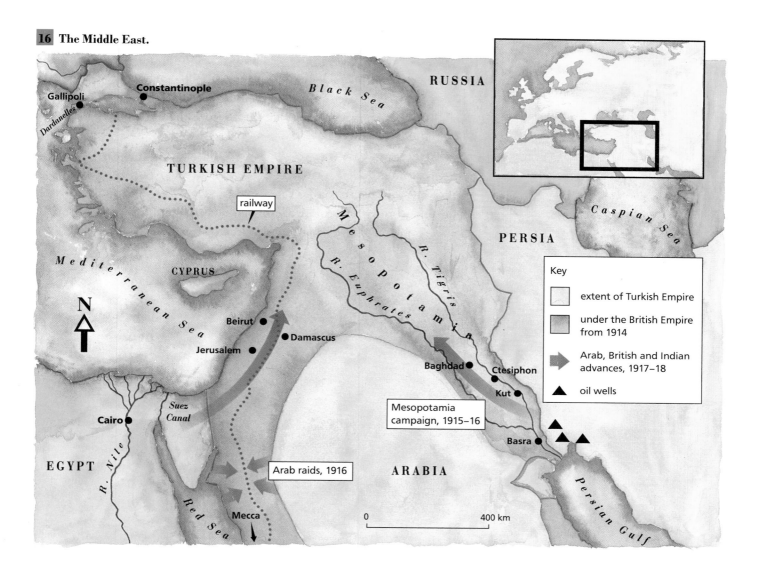

Key

☐ extent of Turkish Empire

▨ under the British Empire from 1914

➔ Arab, British and Indian advances, 1917–18

▲ oil wells

Mesopotamia campaign, 1915–16

Arab raids, 1916

railway

1 **Why do you think the Turkish Empire was crescent-shaped in the south?**

2 **Name the countries where you would find these towns and cities today: Basra; Baghdad; Kut; Jerusalem; Beirut; and Damascus.**

that they would support independence for the Arab peoples if they revolted against the Turks. In April 1916 Hussein's son, Prince Feisal, began the revolt with help from a British officer, T. E. Lawrence ('Lawrence of Arabia'). Feisal's men became specialists in guerilla warfare, especially in blowing up Turkish trains.

1 Why was cavalry used more often in the Middle East than in France?

2 Could Britain have fought the Turks without troops from the British Empire?

3 Why do you think Britain put so much effort into driving the Turks from the Middle East?

The collapse of the Turkish empire

In 1917 the British gathered large armies in Egypt and Mesopotamia for two marches north (see map, source 16). The Mesopotamian Army captured Baghdad. The Egyptian Army, along with Feisal's Arad force, captured Jerusalem, Beirut and Damascus. By October 1918 the Turks had been driven out of the Middle East.

Before the war, Germany had seized a number of territories in Africa. These new colonies were scattered among the colonies of other European powers. None were of great importance to Germany's war effort, but the British took the opportunity to drive the Germans from the continent. By 1916 all the German colonies in Africa had been captured by the British.

17 Indian cavalry charging against the Turks in Palestine in 1918. Painting by F. A. Stewart, 1918.

4 How did capturing the German colonies in Africa strengthen the position of the other European countries there?

5 How do sources 16 and 18 help to explain why the Great War later became known as the First World War?

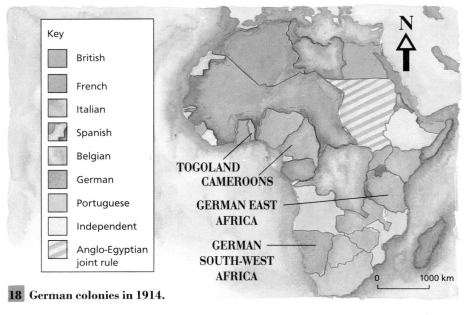

Key

British
French
Italian
Spanish
Belgian
German
Portuguese
Independent
Anglo-Egyptian joint rule

TOGOLAND
CAMEROONS
GERMAN EAST AFRICA
GERMAN SOUTH-WEST AFRICA

0   1000 km

18 German colonies in 1914.

World War and the Western Front

A new offensive and new tactics

Up to 1917 the Great War was mainly a European conflict, with some fighting over colonies alongside. In April 1917 it became more truly a world war when the United States joined in (see page 63). Germany now had to face the fact that freshly trained US soldiers would be shipped to France at the rate of around 150,000 a month from the end of the year.

Then, in 1917, events in Russia also took a dramatic turn. There was a revolution, and the Tsar (Emperor) was forced to abdicate in March. Later, in November 1917, the Bolsheviks (Communists) seized power. In February 1918 the Bolsheviks signed a treaty with Germany and Austria. They agreed to stop fighting in return for handing over large territories in the west of the old Russian Empire.

This was good for Germany. The surrender of Russia meant that Germany could now move soldiers from the Eastern Front to France. Germany could concentrate all its efforts on the Western Front. If German soldiers could break through the trenches, they might crush the British and French before the American Army had become battle-hardened.

That was the aim of General Ludendorff's 'spring offensive' which re-opened a war of movement.

A huge number of guns and supplies were assembled. The German offensive opened with a massive five-hour bombardment on 21 March 1918.

19 **War in 1918.**

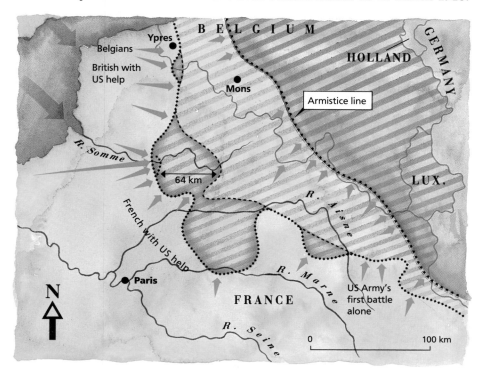

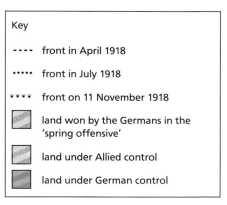

Key

- - - -   front in April 1918

• • • •   front in July 1918

▼ ▼ ▼   front on 11 November 1918

land won by the Germans in the 'spring offensive'

land under Allied control

land under German control

The artillery no longer tried to destroy trenches. Instead, with the help of sound-tracking machines and wireless, it targetted British and French guns. Small and well-equipped groups of German soldiers were gathered into attacking forces. These groups moved swiftly to weak points in the enemy's lines. The British and French were badly battered by the attacks, and casualties were high.

The tide turns

The new tactics forced the British and French to retreat up to 64 kilometres by July 1918. Trench warfare was over. But the Allied generals were prepared to use the same tactics and, unlike the Germans, they had forces of new improved tanks. Some 250,000 extra troops were sent from Britain; many of the soldiers were only 18. The US Army in France had grown to 2 million by July. On 8 August the counter-attack began with what General Ludendorff called the 'black day of the German Army'. On that day, his men had to face British, French, American, Canadian and Australian troops, as well as 2,000 Allied aircraft and 430 tanks. The Germans lost 27,000 soldiers and most of their guns in the battle. In the next month the British alone fired more than 8 million shells, often without any German fire in reply.

Armistice

In September, General Ludendorff told the Kaiser that Germany would be utterly defeated unless they could arrange a cease-fire (or armistice) while German armies were still in France.

The Allies said they would agree if Germany left all the countries it had occupied, hand over its arms and most of its railway stock, together with all its fighting and merchant navies. But they said they would not sign an armistice with the Emperor.

In September no German leader would have dared tell the Kaiser to leave his throne. By November things were different. Britain's sea blockade had worked so well that most Germans were near starvation. Prices were shooting up. Soldiers' letters told of terrible shortages of arms and food at the Front. All over the country there were riots and strikes.

The German Navy Commander ordered the High Seas Fleet to sail from Kiel in a last desperate attempt to win the war. The sailors mutinied. The Kiel mutiny was followed by mutinies among troops in Germany. The trouble spread to Berlin. Socialist leaders set up a new government which forced the Kaiser to abdicate. He took a train to exile in Holland while the new Government sent officials to sign the armistice.

On 11 November, the officials arrived in Paris to sign the agreement to stop fighting. At 11.00 a.m. that day the guns fell silent.

20 British infantry go to battle, September 1918.

1 Explain how you would know the photograph (source 20) was taken in 1918 and not 1917.
2 Was 8 August a 'black day' for the Germans just because of their losses in the battle?
3 Suggest how British soldiers might have felt when they passed through Mons in November.

Review and Assessment

1 In 1914, Britain sent a small army to help the French. *Punch* had warned (see source 8, page 12) that Britain would end up joining a 'general scrap all over the European map'. Between 1915 and 1917, Britain's involvement in the fighting in Europe and the rest of the world grew enormously. Use information in Chapter 6 to list what you think are the major reasons for Britain's growing involvement.

2 After the Battle of the Somme and Passchendaele, many people criticised Haig and other generals for sacrificing many hundreds of thousands of soldiers' lives. Write a speech or a newspaper article in which a supporter of the generals defends the way they ran the war on the Western Front in 1916 and 1917.

3 The Imperial War Museum in London held two special exhibitions. One gave visitors a chance to walk through a reconstruction of the trenches on the Western Front in the First World War. The other helped visitors to experience a reconstruction of bombing ('blitz') in British cities in the Second World War.

   a Explain how these two exhibitions reflect the differences between the First World War and the Second World War.

   b Give examples of how the experience of infantry soldiers in the trenches does not explain some important aspects of fighting on the Western Front.

4 There are five battlefield pictures in this chapter (sources 4, 9, 10, 17 and 20). For each one, write three questions to help future students to use it to increase their understanding of the aspect of the Great War it deals with. The questions should help the student to understand the differences between (i) the fighting in 1917 and in 1918, and (ii) the fighting in Europe and in the Middle East.

7 Counting the cost

Peace at last

When the fighting stopped, people reacted in different ways as the following sources show.

A woman from London wrote to her husband in France:

> **1** *11 November, 1918*
>
> *My Dear Arthur,*
> *. . . Isn't everything ripping! I am so happy!! You can imagine what a relief it was to know that the Armistice was signed . . . Everyone closed down . . . Every vehicle was chartered [hired], private cars, taxis, down to a brewer's dray [cart], including buses, government lorries of every description, and were packed with people making merry with rattles, bells, anything that made a noise. The great place was to sit on the top of the taxi . . .*

Letter from Marie Pankhurst to Corporal Pankhurst, November 1918

Many soldiers' letters and memories show that they responded to the armistice in a quite different way. As an old man, Corporal Pankhurst remembered the reactions of some soldiers:

> **2** *When we'd nearly finished the food I said to them casually, 'The war's over at 11 o'clock this morning.' Somebody said, 'Yeah?' Somebody else said, 'Go on!' They just went on eating! There was no jumping for joy or dancing around. We were so war weary that we were just ready to accept whatever came. When I read of the dancing in the fountains in Trafalgar Square and men riding on top of taxi-cabs . . . my mind always goes back to us few men and the way we took the news.*

Quoted in L. Macdonald, *1914–18*, 1988

1 When Corporal Pankhurst came home from France, how might he have tried to explain the soldiers' feelings to his wife?

BRITAIN AND THE EMPIRE 1914 – 18	
Britain (incl. Ireland)	702,410
India	64,441
Australia	59,330
Canada	57,843
New Zealand	57,843
South Africa	7,121
West Indies	507
Civilians	1,117
Merchant seamen	14,661

3 Britain and Empire: war dead.

Remembering the dead

In Britain, around one in every fifteen men aged between 18 and 50 had died. Their names can be found on 40,000 parish memorials in public places, and nearly another 60,000 on walls inside churches, offices, schools and other buildings.

Many thousands of soldiers died, unidentified, in the mud of Flanders and northern France. On 11 November 1920, the body of an unnamed soldier, was taken as a representative of all those who had died in the war. His body was brought back from the battlefields and buried in Westminster Abbey, as the Unknown Warrior.

5 The battlefield memorial at Thiepval in northern France, the scene of much heavy fighting. 70,000 British and 830 South Africans died here. Their names are on the crosses but their true graves are not known. Many French soldiers also died here.

4 The Empire's memorial: the Cenotaph (or empty tomb) at Whitehall in London. A wood and plaster model was put up for the victory parade by troops of the Empire in 1919. It was replaced by this stone version in 1920.

2 Most memorials had a committee to collect the funds and to decide on the design. Suggest what was in the mind of the people who ordered the memorial at Thiepval (source 5).

3 Edward Lutyens, the architect of the Cenotaph (source 4), decided there should not be a cross on it. Why do you think he decided this?

1 What does your local war
  memorial tell you about war
  losses in the community. Are
  there any people with the same
  name? What does this suggest?

2 If the branch of the forces is
  given, what does it tell you
  about the regiment or battalion
  men joined?

3 If dates are given, can you work
  out whether men were part of
  the BEF or soldiers of the New
  Army. Did men die in large
  numbers at the same time?
  What does this suggest?

4 What does the design of the
  memorial and the inscriptions
  tell you about the people who
  had it set up?

5 Are there any women's names?
  Where do they appear?

6 Many war memorials have an
  addition for the Second World
  War (1939–45). What do the
  inscriptions tell you about
  differences from the Great War.

There were other ways of keeping the memory alive. King George V was told that South Africa had held a two-minute silence everyday through the war. He liked the idea and suggested it for the first anniversary of Armistice Day on 11 November 1919. Today, the anniversary is still marked by a two-minute silence at 11 o'clock, the hour when the fighting stopped.

In 1921 the British Legion was formed, an organisation for all ex-servicemen and women. When Douglas Haig died (in 1928), a fund was set up in his memory to help the British Legion find work and homes for disabled soldiers and their families. Some made poppies in British Legion workshops to keep alive the memory of those who died. Soldiers who had fought in Flanders and northern France never forgot how quickly poppies grew and flowered on the ground they had fought over. For a lifetime after the war, the sight of crippled ex-soldiers was an everyday reminder of the need for the Haig Fund. Few of the people who fought in the war are alive today. But the British Legion continues to provide poppies for the Remembrance Appeal (or 'Poppy Day') in November each year, as a reminder of those who died for their country in the Great War, and later wars too.

6	Great War pensions paid in 1939	
	Amputees (people who have had limbs removed)	11,360
	Useless arms and legs	90,000
	Blind or partly blind	10,000
	Deaf from explosives	11,000
	Head injuries	15,000
	Shell-shock	28,200
	Effects from gas	41,000
	Heart disease	38,000
	Rheumatism from trenches	28,000
	Other severe wounds	32,000

From L. Macdonald, *Roses of No Man's Land*, 1980

Studying local war memorials

It is likely that your nearest war memorial is no more than a few kilometres away. You might like to investigate it. You could pose questions like the ones on the left.

As well as the sight of war memorials, and the war-wounded, there were other small reminders of the war years. Their beginnings were often forgotten. For example, day-time closing for pubs continued until the 1980s (see page 69). In 1914, cinemas and theatres began to play the national anthem at the end of shows, and this went on until the 1970s. Gold coins were replaced by bank notes in 1914 and they never came back. Savings certificates continued after the war had ended. Wrist-watches first became popular in the trenches and soon replaced pocket watches for most people after the war. The length of women's skirts went up and then down, but never again reached their pre-war length. Some factory women got used to wearing trousers for the first time, as they were easier to work in than skirts. And zip fasteners, a wartime invention, have had a lasting effect too.

7 How many people could vote in 1918? How much had the electorate increased since 1910?

8 Explain how both 'heroes' and 'heroines' gained from the *Representation of the People Act* of 1918. Do you think the changes support the statement that the Act made Britain a much more democratic country?

The war effort: were women rewarded?

The vote at last

Women had played a key part in the war effort (see Chapter 4, pages 48–52). For a time they narrowed the gap between what was thought to be the place of men and women in society. Many women expected this to continue in the post-war world. But in political rights and in the work-place they were only partly successful.

Women Suffragists had been campaigning since the 1880s for the right to vote. Just before the war, though, it was the Suffragettes who regularly hit the headlines. The Suffragettes were a group of women who used more extreme and sometimes violent methods to draw attention to the cause of votes for women. They were determined to win publicity, even if it meant going to prison for setting fire to pillar boxes, smashing windows or interrupting public meetings. Many had the courage to go on hunger-strike time after time for their beliefs.

Suffragettes and Suffragists had male supporters – but before the war there were never enough in Parliament to pass a law giving the vote to women. In 1915, women saw an opportunity to make their case again. Hundreds of thousands of men had lost their right to vote as householders and lodgers because they had left their homes to join the Army. The Government needed a new law to give the vote back to these 'heroes'. Suffragists argued strongly that women's war efforts had earned them political rights too. The politicians were slowly convinced. In 1918, Parliament passed the *Representation of the People's Act*. This was the first act to give votes to women in Britain. Women over the age of 30 could vote if they were householders, wives of householders, or fulfilled certain other property qualifications. The Act made Britain a much more democratic country, although women over the age of 21 still had to wait until 1928 for the vote.

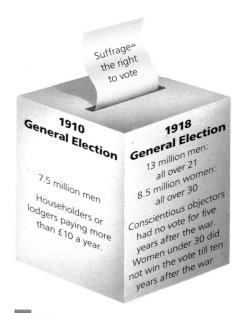

Suffrage= the right to vote

1910 General Election — 7.5 million men — Householders or lodgers paying more than £10 a year.

1918 General Election — 13 million men: all over 21 — 8.5 million women: all over 30 — Conscientious objectors had no vote for five years after the war. Women under 30 did not win the vote till ten years after the war.

7 Who could vote?

1 The man in the cartoon (source 8) is the Prime Minister, Herbert Asquith. Explain what the suffragette is asking him to do.

2 Women had fought for the vote for nearly forty years. Does the evidence here suggest that women 'earned' the suffrage, or that they were given it as a result of their campaigning?

3 Suggest two different kinds of reason why women under 30 were not given the vote in 1918.

4 Why do you think conscientious objectors were not given the vote in 1918?

8 Front page of the suffragist newspaper *Votes for Women*, 26 November 1915.

"Votes for Women," November 26, 1915.   Registered at the G.P.O. as a Newspaper.

The War Paper for Women

VOTES FOR WOMEN

OFFICIAL ORGAN OF THE UNITED SUFFRAGISTS

VOL. IX. (Third Series), No. 408.   FRIDAY, NOVEMBER 26, 1915.   Price 1d. Weekly (Post Free 1½d.)

VOTES FOR HEROINES AS WELL AS HEROES

CHIVALRY : "Men and women protect one another in the hour of death. With the addition of the woman's vote, they would be able to protect one another in life as well."

(The Anti-Suffragists used to allege, as one reason for refusing women the protection of the vote, that women were already protected by men's chivalry—as in a shipwreck, when the women are always saved first. When the hospital ship Anglia went down, last week, the women nurses refused life belts, saying, "Wounded men first.")

9 *Our armies have been saved and our victory assured by the women in the munitions factories.*

E. S. Montagu, Minister of Labour, 22 May 1916

10 *Time was when I thought that men alone maintained the State. Now I know that men alone never could have maintained it, and that henceforth the modern State must be dependent on men and women alike.*

J. L. Garvin, Editor of *The Observer*, 1916

Opportunities at work

Many politicians and employers praised women's work during the war. However, few believed that they should be allowed to compete for jobs on equal terms with men as they came back from the Army. By 1921 the proportion of women among the workforce had fallen to exactly the same figure as in 1911. The only real gain in women's employment was in clerical work where the proportion of females was 45 per cent compared with 21 per cent in 1911. Transport, engineering, and all forms of skilled work were once again jobs where employers looked for male workers. The views in these two extracts help to explain how this came about:

11 *It by no means follows that because women can do men's work therefore they should be allowed to do it. Nor does it follow that because women are willing and steady workers that therefore they should be employed in factories . . . the employment of women is only desirable where the supply of men is deficient* [lacking].

Engineer, 14 November 1919

12 *There is no reason to feel sympathetic towards the young person who has been earning 'pin money'* [money to spend on extra, non-essential things] *while the men have been fighting, nor the girls who left women's work, to which they could return without difficulty, to take the places of soldiers who have now come back.*

Southampton Times, 12 July 1919

5 Discuss sources 11 and 12 from the point of view of a family in 1919 which includes a father and son who have been in the Army, and the son's sister and fiancée who have been doing war-work in a munitions factory.

The Treaty of Versailles 1919

Chapter 1 shows that the people of Europe drifted into war for two main reasons. One was the distrust between France and Germany over the question of Alsace-Lorraine. The other was the desire of different groups of people within the Austro-Hungarian Empire (as well as the Russian Empire) to set up their own nation-states.

The most obvious consequence of the war was the huge number of Europeans killed. But did the peace-makers solve any of the problems that had troubled Europe before 1914 – and if so, for how long?

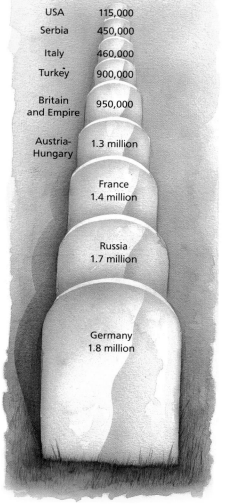

USA 115,000
Serbia 450,000
Italy 460,000
Turkey 900,000
Britain and Empire 950,000
Austria-Hungary 1.3 million
France 1.4 million
Russia 1.7 million
Germany 1.8 million

13 War dead. 1914–18.

1 Which of the new countries were formed from the following old empires: a) German Empire; b) Austro-Hungarian Empire; c) Russian Empire?

2 Which of the old empires in Europe lost *most* land?

The fate of Germany

As soon as fighting stopped, German troops moved out of Belgium and France while the victorious Allies sent troops to occupy Germany up to the Rhine. They also kept up the sea blockade so that Germany remained at near starvation. The occupation and blockade were intended to give the Allies the whip-hand when it came to laying down the terms of the peace treaty.

Between January and June 1919, leaders of the Allies met at Versailles, near Paris, to decide on the terms of the treaty Germany would have to sign. The French in particular were in no doubt that Germany was the aggressor, the country which was alone responsible for the war. So the Treaty laid down that Germany must pay massive war damages, or 'reparations', give up territory to its neighbours, and remain militarily weak for ever. The new German Government protested at these harsh terms but it had no choice. On 28 June 1919, two German minor officials signed the Treaty of Versailles in the presence of the leaders of the victorious countries (see source 16).

14 A new Europe, 1919.

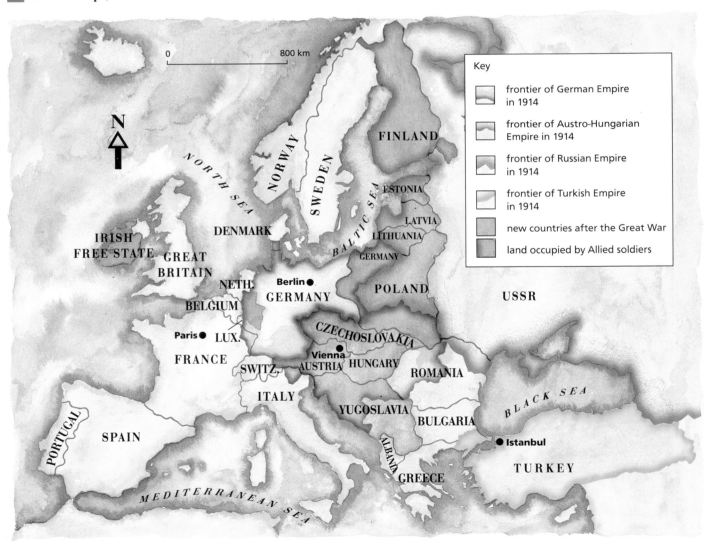

Redrawing the map

The peace-makers also tried to sort out Europe's other causes of unrest. They signed a separate treaty with Austria-Hungary. The Austro-Hungarian Empire had collapsed at the end of the war, and the Emperor had given up his throne. The treaty recognised the new independent countries in east Europe. The Serbs were now united with the Bosnians and other Slav people in a new country called Yugoslavia ('land of the southern Slavs'). This country lasted until 1991.

Another empire which was a casualty of war was the Russian Empire. In 1917 there was a revolution in Russia, and the Tsar was forced to abdicate. The hardships of war and defeats on the Eastern Front were important causes of the upheaval in Russia. A few months later, in November 1917, the Bolsheviks (Communists) seized power – which they were to hold on to until 1991. But between 1919 and 1921 the new Communist government was so weak that parts of the old Empire broke away, setting up independent states such as Latvia, Lithuania and Estonia, or joining with other countries such as Poland and Romania.

Key

1 Alsace-Lorraine back to France
2 Polish 'corridor'
3 no troops in Rhineland
4 not to unite with Austria

5 no submarines only 6 battleships
6 no Air Force no tanks only 100,000 soldiers
7 to pay huge war damages or 'reparations'

15 German war losses.

3 Look back at the illustration on page 8 (source 3). Suggest or sketch a theme for a German poster showing people standing on the Rhine in 1920.

4 Suggest reasons why:
a) Germany was forbidden to unite with Austria;
b) Poland was given a 'corridor' of land;
c) Germany was not allowed submarines, tanks or an air force;
d) French soldiers occupied the Rhineland?

5 What evidence is there that the Allies *blamed* Germany for starting the war?

6 Locate Serbia and Alsace-Lorraine on the map. What had become of these two trouble-spots of 1914?

7 How would you describe the war aims of these countries in 1914: Germany; France; Serbia; Austria-Hungary; Britain? For each country suggest how far they a) succeeded and b) failed.

8 What do you think would be the aims of France; Germany; and the Soviet Union in the 1920s and 1930s?

16 The signing of peace in the Hall of Mirrors, Versailles, 28 June 1919. Painting by William Orpen.

The League of Nations

No one was sure that these new arrangements would last, or that other disputes would not threaten the peace of Europe and the world. The Great War had been so devastating: people agreed that a war like it must never be allowed to happen again. But how could war be prevented? Woodrow Wilson, the American President, pushed hard for a new international body to deal with boundary disputes and acts of aggression in the future. The League of Nations was set up in 1920 and became an important part of the peace settlement. Its standing in the world was soon weakened, though, because the United States Congress refused to agree that their country should be a member. After the sacrifices of the war, many American politicians preferred that their country should isolate itself from quarrels thousands of kilometres away from home.

The League of Nations was, however, involved in the re-settlement of other pre-war empires in the Middle East and Africa. It gave Turkey's Arab colonies and Germany's African colonies to other powers to look after or 'oversee'. These colonies became 'mandate territories' until their people were 'ready' for independence. Britain's mandates were Palestine, Jordan and Iraq and Tanganyika (now Tanzania). France was granted Lebanon and Syria. South Africa took charge of South-west Africa (now Namibia). The mandates were not welcomed by the people of these places who found themselves ruled as colonies, rather than having the independence they had hoped for.

The work of the peace-makers

The painter William Orpen had been a war artist since 1917. He respected the soldiers whose struggles he painted, but he distrusted the politicians who were gathered at Versailles. To him they were just the 'frock's – the men in frock-coats who were only interested in their countries' political interests, and not the ordinary people:

17 *It was all over. The 'frocks' had signed the Peace! The Army was forgotten. Some dead and forgotten. Others maimed and forgotten, others alive and well but equally forgotten.*

W. Orpen, *An Onlooker in France, 1917–19*, 1921

Was that view fair? Was the Army forgotten? Many British soldiers thought so. They had made victory over Germany possible. Yet when they came home, many found they could not get jobs in the years after the war.

Britain was now much weaker economically. The war had given a sharp downward jolt to Britain's standing in world industry and trade. Before 1914 it was a leading industrial power, although it was beginning to lose ground to Germany and the USA. During the war, American industry boomed from sales to Britain and France. The United States lent massive sums of money to

1 **What happened in May 1940?**

2 **Discuss the link between source 2 on page 7 and source 18 below.**

Britain which had to be repaid. What was more, the war had allowed countries such as India and Japan four or five years when they could develop their own industries instead of buying from factories in Britain. In 1918, British industry was facing problems arising from a loss of overseas market which few employers or workers had forseen in 1914.

The army was 'forgotten' in another way too. In post-war Britain there was a widespread feeling that never again should the country get involved in a European war. The Great War should be the 'war to end all wars'. The Army was cut to the size it was in 1914, and, the RAF limited to a few squadrons. They were seen as a force just big enough to deal with trouble-spots in the Empire or the new mandates in the Middle East.

The French, too, wanted to forget the war. Instead of the *élan et cran* – fighting spirit and guts – of 1914, they now built up a defensive army behind the 'Maginot line'. This was a massive stretch of concrete gun-posts and tank traps along their eastern frontier.

Unfortunately, Corporal Hitler did not forget. He had served as a despatch runner in the German Army during the war. On the day the Armistice was signed he was in hospital recovering from blinding by mustard gas. Fifteen years later, in 1933, he was to become Chancellor of Germany. Five years after that, Germany had built up a massive army and air force, tanks, aircraft and submarines. Its troops had marched into the Rhineland, and Austria had been forced into a union with Germany. Europe was poised once more for war.

PEACE AND FUTURE CANNON FODDER

The Tiger: "Curious! I seem to hear a child weeping!"

18 Cartoon from *The Daily Herald*, 17 May 1919. The 'Tiger' was the nickname of the French Prime Minister, Georges Clemençeau. The men behind him are the American President, Woodrow Wilson, the Italian Prime Minister, Vittorio Orlando, and Britain's Lloyd George. A French child born in 1919 would be part of the 'class' who were trained and ready for conscription in 1940.

Review and Assessment

1 Events such as the Great War are important because of what happened and for the way in which they affected people's lives and still affect people's opinions today. Do people's opinions come from what actually took place, or what they think happened? Carry out a survey of a number of adults: either by yourself or as a group. First, decide on the questions you would like to ask such as:

- Why was the war fought?
- What was the most important part of the war?
- How did it change Britain?

For your survey, follow these steps:

a Write out your survey questions.

b Ask the questions and note down (or record) the answers.

c Make a summary of the answers.

d Compare the answers with what you have learned from your study.
   Include these points:
   (i) A list of 'facts' which do not match the evidence you have seen in this book or elsewhere. Explain how the evidence could alter what you were told.
   (ii) A list of aspects of the war which were not mentioned by the people you asked. Explain whether you think the missing aspects were important or not.
   (iii) A list of opinions you have been given about the war. For each opinion say why it could or could not be supported by the evidence.
   (iv) A list of the ways in which the people you spoke to got their information (from stories in the family, television, etc.)

2 Make notes about this book. Is it fair and reliable? Which important topics have been missed out?